Hi, my name is Cleveland Brown. I am the author of this book as well as the author of *Moonshine and Living in The Deep South*. This is my father who is on the back cover of this book. His name is Jetty Brown, a hardworking man. He owned two or three businesses in pulpwood logging and medical transport business from the early 70s to the early 90s. He was a fine businessman and left a long work history behind him. As his son, it gives me great honor to dedicate this book to him in his memory.

He was born in the deep South and it was harder for African Americans to start a business because they had to go through so much to get a loan. This is why we no longer have any more African American farmers in the South. It should not be this way. I am no farmer.

I know he is looking down on me from heaven smiling and saying tell the truth son, that's what I always taught you, to tell the truth.

Living in the Deep South is Hard and Dangerous

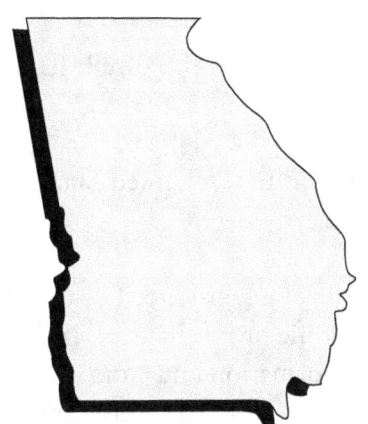

By Cleveland Brown

Wake Forest, NC
www.scuppernongpress.com

Living in the Deep South is Hard and Dangerous

By Cleveland Brown

©2018 The Scuppernong Press

First Printing

The Scuppernong Press
PO Box 1724
Wake Forest, NC 27588
www.scuppernongpress.com

Cover and book design by Frank B. Powell, III

All rights reserved. Printed in the United States of America.

No part of this book may be reproduced or transmitted in any form or by any means, electronic or mechanical, including photocopying, recording, or by any information and storage and retrieval system, without written permission from the editor and/or publisher.

International Standard Book Number ISBN 978-1-942806-17-2

Library of Congress Control Number: 2018955212

Contents

Preface .... *i*

1 — Living in the Deep South 1

2 — Hard Times 7

3 — Changes 13

4 — Poor and Black 17

5 — Open Season 23

6 — Past Struggles 29

7 — Our Legacy 45

8 — Murders in the Deep South 59

9 — Hope for the Future 73

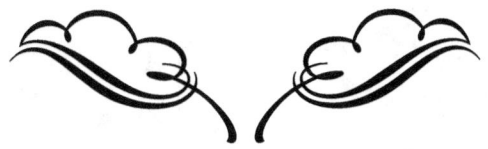

Preface

This book is about Cleveland Brown's experiences as a black man living in the deep South, more particularly, Ashburn, Georgia. Ashburn, Turner County, has consistently scored in the lower one-third as being among the poorest counties in Georgia.

Mr. Brown has a long list of beliefs about race relations in the South which readers will want to consider.

You will quickly notice there has been a minimum amount of editing of Mr. Brown's writing. The intention is to present his writing as a true reflection of him. You will learn that rember means remember, thaire means there or their, theay or thay means they, and so on. It is common for the Mr. Brown to write in sentence fragments.

Cleveland Brown was born November 2, 1937, in Ashburn, Georgia, the only child of Jetty Brown and Arlene Brown. He was raised in Sibley, Georgia, during his early days and in Ashburn, Georgia, at the Stevens Street Projects during his Eureka High School days. As a teenager he helped his father make moonshine on the Williams farm in Sibley, Georgia, before they moved to Ashburn.

As an adult, Cleveland worked in several areas in north Georgia, but later he returned to his hometown to live. To his disappointment, he found race relations in Ashburn had not changed. Cleveland will present his thoughts about today's black youth, small town law enforcement, and who should be educating the African American child, among other subjects relevant to blacks living in the deep South in this small volume.

Cleveland was married to Alma LeBon Brown for 29 years. She passed away in 1997. Cleveland has two daughters, Amery Brown and Michelle Vail. He has two grandsons, Tyrese Vail and Marcus Tukes, from his daughter Michelle.

This is Cleveland's second book following his first, *Moonshine and Living in the Deep South*. He is currently working on his third book.

1

Living In The Deep South

Living in the deep South is hard and dangerous. Being black in the South is a hard life. I know because I was born down here where in the early fifties, blacks had to go to the white man's back door. He worked for him. Sometimes his wife work in their house and even cook their food. I can remember when I was growing up down here my grandmother would send me over to a white lady's house to buy some milk from her. She would always tell me, don't go to the front door. Go to the back door. I would sometime ask my grandmother why do I have to go to the back door? She would say, boy do what I told you. It was a hard life blacks were overworked and under paid. The same thing is going on in 2015. Things ain't too much better when I was a teenager growing up in the South Georgia. I can remember we had to drink out of different water fountains. Some would say (colored) and the other would say (white only) and the bathrooms would say the same we was told what we could not do and what we could. Black men have always been disrespected by white men in the South. The white man has told lies to his children that the blacks are no good. That all black are alike. That is a lie. All blacks are not alike. They say that we are lazy and won't work. Blacks are the ones that built this country with sweat and blood. In the white man walks his country. That is a lie. The white man has always wanted everything ever since they came over here from England. He has never had a country this belonged to the Indian.

I would say in the late forties, some were like as early as 47-48-49. You had a lot of sharecroppers and some working on the farm. But they were mostly black. You had some poor whites working on the farm. But believe they caught more hell than the blacks. Black then the black man had to plow that mule from sun up to sun down. The black man has caught hell ever since his existence in the South even in the 1800s and 1900s he has beaten and been lynched by the white man. Even our women was raped. Even if they would not submit to them, they would kill them. This is what it was in the South. Back in the 50s and

60s, blacks in some part of the South was terrorized by the KKK with crosses were burned in some people's yard. Black churches were burned back then. Like they are being burned today.

In 2015, all of my uncles that lived in the South was sharecroppers. But some was smart and made their way up North. When I told my daughter about how I was when I was growing up here in Ashburn, she said, Dad you got to be kidding. I said no. She said cannot believe this. I said baby this is history. I ask her when she was going to school did her teachers teach them about black history. My daughter told me the only ones black they talk about for black history was Rosa Parks and Dr. King, C. J. Walker and Jackie Robinson. I call that poor black history. I know that we had more blacks than that. You see that is all they want to tell the class because now it is integrated. You see the white kids are in class with the black kids and the white teachers do not want the white kids to know what their grandparents and great grandparents done back then. But God know what they done and he will deal with them. People don't understand how hard living in a country as a black man that you hope build to be not recognized. Disrespect and called niggers behind your back. People it's a hard life to lie. Have you heard the song about smiling face's tell lies? That is true. My dad told me son be careful with white people. They smile out both sides of their mouth. You know they say a race with no past has no future. We have a past. I lived through it. I am a witness. I have been black three times. I have been a black baby, a black boy and black man. So I know how it is to be a black man in the deep South being a teenager and a young man. Down here, trust me I know. When I was a teenager my grandparents would tell me when she would send me uptown or to the store, son stay in your place. I did not know what she was talking bout until I become older. I went to the store one day and said yes to the man in the store. He looked and said nigger you say yes sir to me. I going to tell your grand mammy when she come up here. It was bad growing up here. Black history is our heritage and unless we as black parents teach our kids at home because the white teachers are not going to do it. Because they are in the South. Firsts of all they don't know it because they has not studied it in college. Can you imagine a white student taking up black history in college? Their parents would not pay for their schooling. You cannot teach what you don't know. I am black I know nothing about white history.

You know after looking back at my growing up here in Ashburn, Turner County, it seem like an adventure or a movie. Things are so different now. You has no more nice police. You has not as many nice white people. Everyone wants to tell you how Ashburn back in the day. But they don't have a clue. I could tell them things that happened in Ashburn would make their hair stand on their heads that they think black people do not know about. But we do. Let me just say this by we blacks being a forgiving race or peoples and God-fearing people we forgive. But we don't forget. When I was growing up here, our parent went to the schools were not mixed lessons. You see the schools were not mixed back then. The black teachers cared about the children back then. You see they knew that we was going to need an education to make it in this country. If we were making bad grades, Mr. Dye or Mr. King would come out to our house and talk to our parents. But seem like the parents of today do not care about their kids. They leave it up to the teachers and they are the wrong ones to leave it up to. If you know what I mean. In the deep South that's just like putting a wolf in a chicken house. But at Eureka, the teachers cared about the black kids. I wish I could say that today, but I cannot I just can't. When we got out of order, Mr. King would take us to our parents. Not to the police. We had real teachers not teachers that was just out there for the money. They would help you, not put you in a special class. You know what? We got a better education than the children of today.

You know growing up in the deep South in the 50s and 60s, blacks had it hard. I know a friend his mother cooked at a café here. He asked me and my cousin and uncle to go up there with him. It was on the front street. Which is now called Main Street. So, by us being young boys we did not know blacks were not allowed to go in the front door. But the waiters met us and said where are you niggers going? Don't you'll know we don't allow any niggers in here? So, my friend told his mother, cooked up there and she replied you'll take your black asses around to the alley. It's a window back there for you'll. That happened here where I grew up. When we would go to get a drink of water from the water fountain, they made sure you know which one to drink from. One would say colored on one and white on the other. This is how we had to live. When I was growing up here in Ashburn, if we went to a white person house we had to go to the back door. If a white woman would go up and pick up the man who take care her yard, who is black, he had to ride in the back seat. He better not get in the front seat with that white woman. You see I seen the good, the bad and the ugly. You see a lot of people today give Ashburn a bad name. You see back then Ashburn did not do anything to anyone today. But if the truth was told about some of the people here that has a lot of land and money. Ashburn's eyes would come open. You see the children and grandchildren has all this land. But don't know how they got it. But you can rest assured that they did not by all that land. You see when I grew up here back in the 50s and 60s, black people some had stores. They had cafés. They had pool halls. Brick masons, Black people had more back then. I don't know what happened. They even owned their farms. They even had taxies here. When you wanted to go somewhere all you had to do is call a cab. We had Burk's Robinson, Burgess, Ousley. All you had to do is call they would be right there. Blacks look out for themselves better back then. They did not depend on the white man back then. I know because a lot of my kin people rented land to farm it. But later, the white man got greedy when the government had some of them in the offices that lend money to the farmers. They unknown to the government they would not let the black farmer have loans to farm with. That is why you don't have but a few black farmers today. People this I think happened in the early 70s and 80s and maybe the 90s. But when those black farmers started filing discrimination law suits, then the government said who, What's going on here? Then a lot of whites lost their jobs behind that. But it's too late for the black farmers. That is why we don't see many black farmers in the deep South today. Some of the same thing is going on today in banks and all other institutions that lend money. They come up with credit scores which the republican congress know that poor blacks don't have good credit scores because you cannot pay your bills out of $7.25 minimum wages.

So, they came up with credit scores. They know poor blacks and poor whites don't have good credit. Why? Because today in 2015 minimum wages are $7.25 so what can you pay with that? You know if you don't know your history. You don't know where you come from. Most young blacks you don't even hear them talk about black history. The problem is they have not been tough at home. They have not been taught in the South. But I fault the parent not the teacher. I am going to share something with you all. Did you know that we had a lot of black inventors? I said early that a race with no past has no future. Our black history must be told. If we as black people do not tell it, it won't be told because white people down in the South don't want it to be known. I did a little research and I come up with a lot of stuff. I found a lot of blacks invented a lot of things but I am just going to name some of them. A.B. Blackburn Railway signal. January 10, 1888, W. F. Burr, Switching device for railways, October 31, 1899. F. M. Jones air conditioning unit July 12, 1949, A Miles Elevator October 11, 1887. I am sure most of our young men and women don't know most of our young kids and the teenagers don't know. So, don't let anybody tell you us blacks don't have a past. Brother, we have one. I know because I grew up in it. You know I know we have one. WE used to go to the field and hoe peanuts and cotton. Now the young people don't know what I am talking bout. What it was back then. They did not have weed killer back then, so we had to hoe it out. We would work from seven in the morning until five in the evening and was not making but three dollars a day.

In the 1950s a minimum wage was 75 cents an hour. My dad worked to a sawmill here in Ashburn. When wages were at $1.00 an hour. The boss said he was not going to pay it. He told dad and the others he would shut the damn mill down before he would pay that, and he did. Do you know it took Georgia a right at sixty years to get to $7.25 an hour? That is why so many of us poor blacks and whites and we have our government to thank for that. And here it is almost 2015 and it is still $7.25 an hour. Down in the South Blacks have always been underpaid. We have been held back from good paying jobs. We have always had a hard time borrowing money at the banks and still is, but I don't think the federal government knows a lot of stuff that's going on in these banks. You know the people that are running these banks in Ashburn and the state got this good old boy system. So, if you black with low credit remember it was not like that. I hear some people say time change, that's not true. Don't change. People do. But you see when I was growing up on the farm we grew just about everything we ate. We had cows, hogs, chickens. We had a garden the only things mother would have to buy was flour. When dad would kill hogs, they would make the lard. I better tell these young peoples what lard is. It is what we call cooking oil. You see when the people back then kill hogs, they would take that fat what they trim from the meat when they cut the meat up. I know you young people's don't know what I am talking about. But all those old schools that come up when I did know what I am talking about. Times was bad back then. But kids just don't know how blessed today they are. You should thank God we have it hard.

Living in the Deep South is Hard and Dangerous

2

Hard Times

We had a new Eureka School. By the 70s, schools all over the South was being integrated. So, by that time our school had over 1,000 students. When they got us in our new school, the first thing they done was change the name to Turner County at Eureka. That was wrong and a lot of other stuff that the white peoples here in Ashburn done. But that wasn't' through. The next thing happen later on they wanted to close the school. I contacted the president of the NAACP and the first thing he said was that the white teachers afraid to teach over there. But we had a problem with that. Because every day after school the white kids would be right back in the black neighborhood. Mostly white girls. Then they came up with the story about some of the building had asbestos. Whatever that is. But listen they move some of the school to Ashburn High which was white at the time. So, what do that tell you bout deep South? Time goes by, but prejudice stays the same. We as a black race are to divided in the South and the white man down here know it. So, he works to keep us that way all he was ever about was to divide and conquer. We have some lacks that will fall in his little traps. But we older blacks know what time it is with those guys. I may sound like its racist but not. I am just telling it like it was down here in the deep South. The only way that anyone can tell what happened down here is you had to live here. People may have painted a picture of the South in the early 50s, 60s and 70s. But it was not good for us blacks. I know because I lived through those in the deep South.

You know some call us it the dirty South. But you know what we is. You see in the early 60s, the South was a little better but not much. Because Ashburn hired its first black police officer in 1967. They are still alive today. But it lasted a while until those guys arrested a white man. They was told they could not arrest a white man. They could pull him over and call a white officer to do the call and a white officer to do the arresting. The two black officers turned in their badges and told their chief if they could not arrest whites just like the blacks, he could have his job. Can you blame those guys? So that prove to you about the South back in the day. During the 60s we have a whole lot of stuff going on. Back then Dr. King and the marchers was doing a lot of marching and being put in jail. Also, blacks were being killed. The police was beating the blacks. They were also spraying them with water and putting the dogs on them. Also burning black churches. People some parts of the South was a living hell for black people. The KKK was burning black's homes and burning crosses on the property and terrorizing the black neighborhood and carrying the same flag they are raising hell about in 2015, the Confederate flag. But we won't talk about it because haven't got there yet. In the 60s was a time all blacks should remember those that was old enough. I can remember and will never forget the things we as blacks in the South had to endure and things that the white man put our parents through and their parents. So, I am telling everyone what you heard about the South is 95 percent true.

    I was talking about the small farmer early, but I could not remember all at that time. And had to go back and put on my thinking cap. I have said the small black farmer was put out of business because he could not get money to farm with and the large farmer did not help any because bought all the land if he could not buy, he rented it. I know all the small black farmers where I live because my uncle was one of farmers that had to give it up. I am going to show you the different when my dad was share cropper and see back then the farmers could tell time by the sun. When the sun shows his face, the farmer has been at it for a couple of hours. I know when my dad was sharecropping, my mother would be up cooking breakfast before daylight. I would still be in bed. Dad would be fixing water to take with him to the field. It would take about an hour to get ready to go to the field. It was fun living on the farm, except those hot 90-degree heat come spring. Dad would say time to plant the summer garden. I liked the fall because I love to shell peas and butterbeans. By the 50s guess what, we had electricity lights. No more oil lamps and wood stoves goodbye. There was always a garden except in the winter but guess what — we had sweet potato hill we could rob. Man, baked sweet potato coming out of steaming with an aroma that singed your nostrils. Nothing is better in the winter than a buttered sweet potato. Just like milkshake on a hot summers most satisfying nothing like living on the farm in the 50s. But if you was black, you lived on the farm you did not catch as much hell as the blacks that lived in the city did. But the white people was not like that. If they did not show it, because knowing my dad like I did, he would not stand for that. He was a good man. But don't rub him the wrong way. If you did, he would let you know

Back in the 60s, blacks had so many rules they had to abide by. Back in the 50s that was worst if we caught a Greyhound bus we had to sit in the back. If a white person got on the bus and there was no seats, the blacks would have to get up and let the whites have their seats. And the blacks had to stand up. People we have had it down here. I can't remember this but grandmother told me that her mother which is my great great-grandmother said they had to run and hide from the white man. To keep from being picked up and taken away and sold as slaves. I can remember my great great-grandmother a little because I was small. Her name was Mary Shin. My dad said she was 80 years old when she passed away in the mid 40s. My grandmother said it was bad for them blacks in the South as time progress things began to get a little better in the late 60s but racism was not done. It still was a lot going on prejudice and hate running around. I don't understand. Why the white people hate us blacks? We have never did anything to them. They got it backwards. We are the race that should be hating all the things that they have done to us since slavery. They have took our land. They have worked us for nothing. We have been lynched by them. Killed by them. Our women have been raped by them. I could go on and on. So, they cannot name one thing that the black race of people done to them. By we being a race of God fearing people and forgiving. God is all about love not hate. How can a race of people hate their black brothers and sisters and go to church?

Every Sunday saying, I love the Lord, but hate their black brothers and sisters? The Bible says you cannot enter the kingdom of heaven. I just want to say to my white brothers and sisters you better change out of all you have done to me and my peoples. I still love you. I don't hate you. I hate the things you do. The things you stand for and most of all the lies that you tell behind them. I know as a black race of people, we have always been hated down here in the deep South. And maybe some parts of the North. I don't know this because I never lived up there. But I can only speak about where I was born and raised up at, but God sit high and look low. He already said what would happen to the ones who harm his peoples. Is it fear? You see as a race of people, we had to live in fear back in those days. But it is slowly changing in the 80s, 90s, but we know change will come. But the one thing we have to do is educate

Living in the Deep South is Hard and Dangerous

our kids about their heritage, their ancestors and we as a black race got to America. We as parents has to do this. No one else will. Our kids need to know who and what happened to great great-grandparents. I know my white brothers has told their kids about us. Which was all lies. My grandmother worked for a lot of white people in Ashburn. In their houses she cooked, cleaned and nursed their kids. She was well known by everybody back then. Her name was Rosa Brown. So, all white people in the South is not haters. I tried to tell my two daughters all that I know about our heritage and our ancestors the best that I could. And what my grandparents told me. We our ancestors did not ask to come over here.

I would like to share a poem about our black history title.

I am going back. I was brought here against my will. I worked for no meaning. I received no pay. Think of the pay didn't receive. Think of the pain. Then feel it. Touch my ears. Think what was hidden from me. They imprisoned my mind into a night without stars. I am bleeding. This wound will never heal until the mass flow of positive energy circulates throughout the mind. That it was hidden from. But in order for me to for gain this power, I must go back. Don't cry. Please don't cry. I cry because my destiny has been hidden from me. You cry because of sympathy for me. But it is not needed. Because I am going back to where storms idolize my power. To where nights are as bright as day to where my knowledge will be shared and advanced to love is great that the most distorted mind can be fine-tuned into a picture so clear. That the blind can see further. To where I am as a king. I didn't ask to come here, but I was forced whenever a man is made to do something against his will then that force that dries him to this is always less than a man. I stayed here and because a part of this, but home is calling. No matter how much pain I went through, I never hated. Instead I laughed. And they thought I was blind, but they couldn't see either. Now my eyes are in tears. But they are forever open. My mind is trapped. But soon as I reach my motherland, the effect of the magi will free it and heal it of all of its mental wounds. When I arrive, I will kneel and thank God the second I touch the mystic soil. Then I will get a handful of this soil and let the grains fall through my open hand and it will be then that the tears will stop, but only of pain because I will cry out happiness when I kiss my brothers and sisters and when I meet the greater ones who will let me know about my father's because here the truth is limited. It is more than a destiny to go there. I must. I have to. Maybe you can. Do you want to go? Do you? Just think about it quickly and remember this. I am coming back. So, if its decided to go and then come back. You will return alone and if you do not go then now is he time to say goodbye to me. Because I am going back. I am going back. Never to return. I am going back.

You know that was something. A classmate of mine gave me that poem when he moved back here. He passed away a few years after he moved back home in Sycamore. He had been around the world. He lived in Africa for nine years. He also married an African woman. He also told me a lot of stuff about our homeland, our kids need to know this. They will never learn this because most of their teachers are white and they are not going to tell them anything about their heritage. I have read history books at the library way back in the 1800s. How the whites always been superior over the blacks. It has always been that the white mans has told blacks what they had to do. Blacks had no rights. They could not vote back then. The white woman was almost like the backs could not vote. The white man in the South always wanted to be the boss. He has always wanted all of the money. All the land. He has always been lazy. Always wanted to live off the black man's labor. That's the way it was in the South back then and almost like it now.

In the deep South, blacks went through hard times. In the South and I think I can tell what I know. I think the black man can tell it and tell the truth. I have read a lot of about us. But a black man was not saying. I just want to ask a question. If you treating a person right you don't need to defend yourself. We have been treated wrong in the South ever since. I am going to let the young black men know something. I have heard a lot of talk about us. A white man was saying that a lot of blacks fought in the Confederate army, that's a lie. I did a research of the war and found a bill was introduced in the Confederate senate in 1865 providing for the enlistment of 200,000 negroes and their emancipation if they remained loyal through the war. Advocates of the measure had the approval of General Robert E. Lee. The enlistment of negroes was very slow. A white man, the Indian say, speak with forked tongue. The few that fought with the Confederacy was killed. Some by the Confederate when blacks were permitted to enlist in the union they did so. The blacks knew that they would still be enslaved if the South won the war. If the Confederates would have won the war, where would blacks be today? I don't know, we can sure would not be slaves you can bet your boots. It might have been another war. So, if anybody tells you that a lot of blacks fought for the Confederate you tell them that's a lie. To go to the library and look it up. Blacks in their right mind is not going to help anybody that held them in captivity. Now we still have some of those house niggers. That's what the masters would call them. But if we had any around in the 60s, 70s which I know we did, but if we would have caught him telling the white man anything back then, he would not be seen anymore.

I cannot understand how someone can hate a race of people for so long that has done nothing to them. We as blacks cannot help because our skin is different from others. I would just like to say to my white brothers be a man and tell your black brother why you hate them. I seen people, black people killed down here in the deep South. Black men have been killed by the police and nothing done about it. What we have in the deep South this KKK in police uniforms with a badge to kill black men. I know time has to change. In the late 80s, 90s you could see the change. But a lot has to be done.

For sure minimum wage has to change in the deep South. I am just going to share some thing with you about our wages in the deep South. I have done some research on the wages. Something we as black people don't keep up with. In 1968 wages was $1.60 an hour. In 1996 $4.75 ok. 1974 $2.00 an hour. In 1997 $5.15 ok, 1975 $2.10 an hour, 2007 $5.85 an hour. What I am trying to say is look at the years between the pay raises. No wonder that we poor black and whites are in poverty and food stamps. I know some peoples might know this and some may not.

One thing that we have down here in the deep South is good old Southern food. Good old fried Southern gold brown chicken. You'll need to come on down here. Yes we have good down here. Don't get me wrong, we also have some good white peoples down here. Me, being a Southern man born down here grew up here in this small town called Ashburn, Georgia, a place some peoples say they never heard of. OK, I will tell you it's about 176 miles South of Atlanta, Georgia. If you on Interstate 75, you will see Ashburn exit. But if you're speeding you will not see it. Because you will be pulled over.

3

Changes

I am not bragging we have more than the good Southern food down here. We have some good-looking girls down here and they are Southern grown. I tell you we have a lot of good stuff down here. We also have some good moonshine whiskey down here too. So, you'll come on down and set a spell here. In the 90s time was better for blacks down here, but you know there is always room for improvement. Let me just go back in time just a bit. You see a lot of young blacks cannot remember the great baseball player Jackie Robinson. Broke the color barrier in sports in 1947. Jackie was born in the deep South. In a place called Cairo, Georgia. The grandson of a slave and a son of a sharecropper. On April 15, 1947, Jackie Roosevelt Robinson forever changed the complexion of major league baseball. Professional sports and life of America. That's the day he became the first black during the 20th century to play in a regular season game. He played with the Brooklyn Dodgers from 1947 until he retired following the 1956 season. He led the Dodgers to six pennants during that 10-year span. Surviving death threats, race baiting from players and fans. Strike threats and being a target for pitchers. In 1947 Robinson was named the National League's most valuable player in 1949. Jackie paved the way for black athletes in this country. He died in October 1972 at age 53. I am going to do something. I am going to step the time to right now to 2015. If it had not been for Jackie Robinson, blacks would not be able to play in no sports today. So, thank you Jackie. Thank you, Robinson and family, moved to Pasadena, California. Robinson reached the pinnacle of his career when he was inducted into the hall of fame in 1962. During the 1940s he fought for better treatment of black soldiers. He was court marshaled for refusing to move to the back of a military bus, but ultimately was acquitted. Silent during the first two years with the Dodgers because of a promise made to owner Branch Rickey, Robinson, starting with his third season, voiced his displeasure about discrimination from other players and umpires. After leaving the game, he supported Richard Nixon during the 1960 presidential campaign when most blacks were democrats. He also worked closely with Dr. Martin Luther King on his nonviolent civil rights reform movement. Robinson probably affected more change with his actions, on and off the field, than any other American. Seven years after he broke baseball's color barriers segregated schools were outlawed by the Brown v. Board of Education decision. Seventeen years later, the 1964 civil rights act was implemented. Some of Robinson's teammates want to share something about Jackie. Williams was a Robinson teammate from 1951 until 1956. He later managed the A's, Angels, Expos, Padres. How many of you guys that is playing sports now think you could have went through what Jackie went through? He was called all kinds of names which I refused to put in my article. Listen guys all of you that's playing sports every now and then think about Jackie and what he had to endure. What he had to listen to and sometime a lot of times hit with that hard baseball. You know what. Just so you guys can play with any team, you want, to stay at any hotel you want to. Jackie could not go to the same hotel with his team. You guys can. Jackie paved the way.

Jackie's friend players thank Jackie for paving the way for them. Dwight Gooden said what Robinson went through has meant a lot to me. I definitely have not forgotten what he did for the game of baseball. The African American athletes and for all minorities really. He has given us the chance to go out there and excel in a game that was not available to us 50 years ago Carter said. Carter is one of baseball's most productive hitters during the past 10 years. Believes racism still exists in the sport 50 years after Robinson broke the color barrier. It's a shame here we are in the 2000s and African American still have to go out and prove themselves. White managers can get fired form one team and suddenly, their names are put into a pool and they end up going to other teams to manage those teams. Why we don't get those opportunities? I look at my manager Cito he was not go the respect that he deserves after winning two world series and out managing both managers in the world series. He has dealt with his in the right manner to get the most from us. But he never has been labeled as a genius. Other guys have been labeled as geniuses that never been to a world series or won one. He won back to back championships and still does not get the respect or recognition and you wonder why. It's not because he does not have the talent. So, you look at other things and realize it must be racially motivated. It is sad to say in this day in age, but it is true. Said Carter who hit the winning home run in the 1993 World

Series against Philadelphia he continued. There are a lot of African American athletes in baseball and football and basketball who have the knowledge and experience and are never given the chance. We are approaching the year of 2000 and this raciest stuff still going on. New York's pitcher David Cone, the American league's representative feels Robinson was an incredible person. He obviously was a very special man. He opened the door for all the best players in the world who are playing on the major league level now and that could not be said back then. A lot of the best players were in the Negro Leagues now and that could not be said back then. And even in Japan Barry Larkin short stop for the Cincinnati Reds since 1986 has been named team captain by Manager Ray Knight of Albany, GA. That's something that never may have occurred if it was not for Robinson. He basically represented the minority community sociologically, He had a tremendous amount of pressure on his back. As did as a baseball player would be reflected on how society accepted the minority race Larkin said. Let's fast forward to 2015. A lot of our young minorities don't know that Jackie Robinson paved the way for them to play sports with any league that would have them. Jackie had to go through a lot of stuff for you to play where you want to and who will let you play. Always remember Jackie was always the best he could be. His name will live forever. And when you are playing any kind of sports think about who paved the way for you to be there. Some of the players came along behind Jackie also hard time, But not as bad as Jackie. He changed the color of the baseball field. He broke the color barriers that took some nerve. Back in 1947, it was real dangerous for African American. Back then the Klan was riding.

    This is 2015 and people have not got over the civil war and the Confederacy that is the same flag was carried in the Confederacy war against an army. That flag is no heritage. It's in the battle against an army that was trying to free black human beings who are enslaved. So what kind of heritage that is. How can a white man in Worth County, Georgia say blacks fought, bled and died? Under the flag when the people that was carrying was killing them and burning them alive. I think the flag represented racism, hate. I think the two white teenagers who organized the rally need to read the history behind the flag you'll carried from Lee County to Dougherty County on July 18, 2015. Without a permit which was against the law. Once again color makes a difference. If you'll had been black you would had went to jail. You see I know we still have some Uncle Tom's that wears a badge and don't forget the house nigger. They all ain't dead. I think the young whites are being misled by their parents and grandparents. Because the grandparents don't want their grandchildren to know that they were a part of what went on in the deep South. That is why they do not teach the real black history in the schools down here in the deep South. But one thing about it will show up. This 2015 and look at the trouble that flag has caused. No good will come out of this. In Atlanta the capital of Georgia a few weeks ago someone displayed small Confederacy flags in a black church where Dr. King pastored. What does that tell you? Is that the way you enjoy our heritage? I can tell all of the young grandparents because they are growing. And you are coming they will soon be gone and you will be left behind. Think about it.

The surrender of the Confederacy was a victory. President Lincoln and his policies. Lincoln had spoken out against slavery. Slavery was abolished after the adoption of the 13th Amendment late in 1865. At no time in the nation's history had a group done so much to shape public opinion and then put it to action. To do bodily harm with them. They had labored unilaterally suffering with them it was a moral crusade. You know that we had a lot of blacks fought in the union army. Why? Because they wanted their freedom. Something that they would not get from the Confederacy and most of them knew this. But still today in this century 2015, they are trying to say a lot of blacks fought with the Confederacy. Which is untrue. Because history does not say that. I says a slim margin. That meant almost none. Someone has been reading the wrong history book. But you know the deep South will not admit it. It got it butt kicked by the North. Down here we as blacks, us older blacks know, but some way we have got to teach the generation of today. They has to know that they has a past. They has got to not to what anyone tell them about black history. If they are not black. Blacks are not rebels. Never has been and never will be. So, do not fool yourself. You are an American (negro) and that's all you are not a Johnnie Reb. You have never rebelled against anything. So be proud of who you are because black is beautiful and don't forget it. Black matches anything. Company 4th United States Colored infantry over 186,000 blacks fought under the Union flag during the civil war. Company E was one of the detachments assigned to guard the nation's capital. So, you see if you had been a rebel and black you would not been given that chance.

4

Poor and Black

I need to fast forward this to 2015. There is so much going on in the deep South about the Confederate flag. Which is nothing but a piece of cloth. Does not hurt anyone. What it's use for is what hurts. When someone displays it like it was done in South Carolina, that what hurts. When the KKK use it their marches. I know and the people who are marching around the deep South with it know what it is used for and what it represents. They can lie all they want to. Blacks know what it represented in the civil war and in the 50s and the 60s nothing has changed. They took the hoods off the KKK and gave them a badge and gun to make it legal to shoot an unarmed black man in the back. How can any judge sit on the bench and justify what I would call murder? Police should be held accountable for their action. If the judges keep letting them off they are not going to stop. 558 civilians have died at the hands of police according to the *Washington Post* which says that officers have been charged in only four cases all of which were captured on video. Three of the cases, the victims were black. While the officers were white, in the fourth, the civilian was also white. The criminal justice system is one of the bastions(?) of blatant racism, pastiche(?) of prejudices, wrongheaded stereotypes and all too human assumptions. The implicit and explicit biases that color black people as dangerous and anti-social tend to let police officers, especially white officers off the hook. Their crimes often go unpunished. Can you remember the trial for the four LAPD Los Angeles cops in the brutal 1991 assault of Rodney King videotaped by a passerby as they repeatedly beat and kicked him?

They were charged with assault with a deadly weapon and use of excessive force. Yet none were convicted in the Simi Valley courtroom. Two of the four, Stacy Koon and Laurence Powell were later convicted after federal authorities charged them with violation of King's civil rights. Now watch this. Still U.S. District court Judge John Davis was clearly sympathetic to the two men, saying that King had contributed significantly to provoking the offensive behavior. While they faced up to 10 years in the prison, he sentenced them to 30 months to 10 years in prison. He sentenced them to 30 months. This why police officers do what they do because they know that the judges are not going to do anything to them. The judges need to be taken off the bench the way they are letting these police officers get away with murder. I never seen anything like this. Police shoot an unarmed man in the back and the judge say "justified." Some way, somehow, some one, must stop these white officers from shooting black men. If someone don't come with a way to stop these officers from murdering these black men, the people are going to take the law in their hands and stop it and I am pretty sure it won't be pretty. But if the justice system does what is supposed to do, all these murders would be locked up and not still riding around with a badge and gun. In order for this to happen, they will have to clean judicial bench and get judges that are not prejudice against blacks. But that's what we have in the deep South.

If you are poor and black in the deep South, you are in trouble. That is why when blacks was a slave in the South, if they got a chance they would try and run away to the North. Some would make it and some would not. Some was caught and refused to go back. They were stripped and beaten to death or burned alive. That is what blacks went through in the early 1800s and 1900s. A black woman was lynched in Loins County, Georgia, May 19, 1918, (Mary Turner) was a thirty-three-year-old African American woman. She was eight months pregnant. Turner and her child were murdered after a public denounced the extra judicial killing of her husband by a mob. Her death is considered a stark example of racially motivated mob violence in the deep South and was referenced by the NAACP Anti Lynching Campaign of the 1920s, 1930s, 1940s. She is on the list of 148 African American women who were lynched in America. There's nothing ever done about her husband's murder or her lynching. That's what the white people in the deep South was doing to the blacks back in those days. This is why young blacks should now their black history. Go to the library they are not going to teach you this in school. You need to know the person's history that is teaching you. And you be around Blacks have been denied decent living all their lives. They have never been given the chance to do what they wanted to do. As grown men, the white man has always addressed them as boy or nigger. He has never in the deep South been respected as a man. The deep South has changed some in 2009 and up but has a lot more changing to do.

The deep South in 2009 through 2015 still has a lot of changing to do in states and peoples. In the deep South some people are tired of the same thing they want changed. But you have that segment of people out there that don't want changes. I have heard a few of those old good boys say it need to go back the way it used to be. So, you see we still has some of those racist people still alive down in the deep South that would take it backwards if they could. I don't care what they do or say, the deep South will never go back to where it came from. I know the blacks are not going back. I have read in newspapers where some racist whites has made that statement but it will never happen in this world. I know there is people out there if they could they would. Because they don't like to see the black and white race get along. Black people is easy to get along with as long as you treat them right, but don't get them wrong. Don't you might have a problem. God created all of his people just the way he wanted them. Red, white, black and brown. So, if anyone has a problem with these colors must see God about it. Why a lot of people hate a certain race of people they don't have God in their life. He said love your brother as you love yourself. You see God is love. He said if you hate your brother, who you see every day and love him God whom you has never seen, you is a lie and will not enter the kingdom of God. So, you see God is just God he is going to judge every man for the work he do. He also said he would do the separation. So, we need to let God do his job. Man has already got everything he put his hand on it and messed it up.

 I would just like to turn the clock in the deep South back to 2015 and back to 2012 and maybe 2011. You see we have had so many murders down here by police officers who are paid by the people they are murdering. I don't understand how the judges can call it justified. When you shoot a man in the back. Just look at what happened in Jacksonville, Florida, on November, 23, 2012. A 47-year-old white male software developer was convicted of attempted murder for shooting into a car full of teenagers after an argument over what he called their "thug music." This man showed no emotions as the verdicts were read. The parents left the courtroom in tears and afterward the parents each left and there was gratitude expressed because of the verdicts. Sunday would have been the teens 19th birthday. The man was charged with fatally shooting a 17-year-old boy from Marietta, Georgia. In 2012 after the argument over loud music coming from the parked SUV occupied by the boy and three friends outside a Jacksonville convenience store.

The man who was white had described the music to his fiancée as thug music. A sentencing date will be set at a hearing next month. Each attempted second-degree murder charge carries a maximum sentence of 30 years in prison. While the fourth charge carries a maximum of 15 on his potentially lengthy sentence, the father of one of the victims said he's going to learn that he must be remorseful for the killing of my son. That it was not just another day at the office. We need more judges like Judge Russell L. Healy. The panel said they were having trouble reaching agreement on the murder charge. He asked them to continue their work. This is how the whites lie when they get caught. He kept escalating to the point where he had no choice to defend himself. What a white lie.

I said it once, now twice, a black man in the deep South has never been respected in the deep South. It don't care how far you go back you will not find a black man respected anywhere. Even on the murder case down in Jacksonville, Florida, where the black kid was murdered. On the jurors there was not one black man on the jury. OK, here is how the 12 jurors who had been sequestered since February 6. Now watch this. Consisted of our white men, four white women, two black women, one Hispanic man and one Asian American woman. Some black leaders expressed disappointment that there were not black men on the jury. Damn right. Why no black men was not on jury? I can tell you why. Because the murder was a white man and they know that a black man will not sway on a jury like the black women. This trial was the latest Florida case. Questions about self-defense and race, coming six months after the man was acquitted in the shooting of the 17-year-old in Sanford, Florida. About 125 miles south of Jacksonville. The Dunn trial was prosecuted by the same state attorney's office that handled that case. The attorney for the man who shot the boy told reporters before the verdict that he believed there was political pressure on the prosecutors and an excess of media attention who wept after the verdict. Said they were grateful for the jury's decision to convict him of attempted murder and would await his retrial. It has been a long road and we are so very happy to have a little bit of closure. You know it is sad to have a child murder about loud music. It is that loud, I am sure the police would have told them to turn it down. You do not take the law into your own hands like this man did.

There will be no rest in this country by the black race nowhere in this country until the law of the land makes all these white policies be held accountable for their actions. If they murder someone they will be punished like anyone else. Such as shooting unarmed blacks or anyone who is not a threat to them. If this does not happen, there will be more. The same people we are paying to protect us are murdering us and this is not right, and the black race of people know this. This is what's going on all over this country. But mostly in the deep South. It's a small town located about 176 miles south of Atlanta. What I call a small town that is being controlled by a few rich whites. It has a lot of unsolved murders and nobody seems to worry about it. I had a cousin that somehow ended up in a pond right alongside of Highway 41 South and nobody has done anything, and nobody has been charged with it. He supposed to have drowned. But there was no water in his body. So, what do that tell you? He was dead before he was put in the water. Another black young man who was born in the deep South and he died here. They say he jumped out in front of an 18-wheeler on Highway 112 about three miles west of this small town. It was said the man was naked and his clothes were folded on the side of the road. Listen this young man was taken to a local funeral home where did not let his parents know anything in about their child had been killed. Someone in this town knows who did these crimes. One of these days someone is going to pay for these crimes. We have a lot of stuff that goes on down here. People down here marching around with that Confederate flag just like they are in the army. They think it's okay for them to keep on marching from town to town and say they are going to march in a black neighborhood. There is no black neighborhood. Blacks live everywhere. So, you are remembering backs of slavery.

The murder case in Jacksonville, Florida, should be a road map for these other cities and states. They are freeing these cops that are shooting blacks in the back. And some even tell lies like he was trying to take my gun, or I was a fear for my life. Or I thought he had a gun. Mr. Dunn tried to tell a lie about those teenagers had a shotgun. In this fiancée's testimony undermined his credibility to back his claim. The fiancée shaking on the witness stand said that Mr. Dunn had not mentioned to her in the night and day that they spent together before his arrest that any of the teenagers had a shotgun. Ms. Rouer was inside the gas station convenience store when the shooting occurred. You see this is the kind of stuff the good old white boys down here in the deep South we more Judge's like Haley. He did not want the same thing to happen in Jacksonville that happen in Sanford six months later and the prosecutor did a good job in this case. Look what happened. These white men in the deep South think they can shoot blacks and its ok. Look. Mr. Dunn who was from out of town visiting left the scene and did not call 911 or the police after the shooting. Instead he returned to his hotel and the next morning drove two and a half hours to his home in Brevard County. The prosecutors said his behavior did not jive with the actions of a man who had fire in self-defense. They also argued that Mr. Dunn had enough time to reflect before shooting which was why they accused him of premeditated murder. Some of these cowards back shooting polices need to get the same time Mr. Dunn got. The police always complain. He was trying to take my gun. Don't you all be trained to be police officers. There will come a time when you cannot get your gun. Don't you all be trained hand to hand combat use your skills. If you are scared, you are in the wrong place. A coward will kill you.

5

Open Season

It is so sad when it is open season on black men in the deep South. Police officers are murdering them. And they aren't even armed. The justice system is broken for the black race. America has turned its back on the black race. It a shame when black's hope builds this country and they are not even appreciated. They are being shot down on the streets of the Southern cities by these out of control police officers and these racist judges don't be anything about tit. The killing in Sanford and New York, Ferguson, Texas, and so on. Those police officers and George Zimmerman should get the same time that Mr. Dunn got for killing the teenagers in Jacksonville. Until we get judges prosecutors to uphold the law and quit trying to protect these racist police officers, the murdering by them will never stop. You have murdering done more to blacks than whites. When people get caught. Listen Dunn in claiming self-defense, testified that he thought he saw a firearm pointed at him from the SUV as the argument escalated. No reason was found in the SUV. The prosecutors argued that Mr. Dunn had fabricated his story about the shotgun to bolster his self-defense claim. The police never found a shotgun, and no witnesses never reported seeing one. The teenagers testified that none of them had a shotgun in the car. That was why no one shot back at Mr. Dunn. The prosecutors said Florida's so called stand your ground provisions under the law Mr. Dunn needed only to have been convinced that he saw a shotgun. Whether or not one was present. According to authorities, Dunn became enraged about the music and ensuing argument. One person walking out of the convenience store said he heard Dunn say you are not going to talk to me like that.

Police must be held to a higher standard and held accountable for their actions. They were charged with assault with a deadly weapon and use of excessive force, yet none were convicted in the Simi valley courtroom. Two of the four Stacy Koon and Laurence Powell were later convicted after federal authorities charged them with violating King's civil rights. Still U.S. District Court judge John Davis was clearly sympathetic to the two men, saying that King had contributed significantly to provoking the offense behavior. While they faced up to 10 years in prison, he sentenced them to 30 months. Now fast forward a quarter century in May 2015, Cleveland police officer Michael Brelo, who is white was acquitted of manslaughter in the 2012 deaths of unarmed black motorist, Timothy Russell and passenger Malissa Williams, after other officers had ceased shooting and Russel had stopped his car he had led the officers on a high-speed chase. Brelo jumped onto the hood of the vehicle and fired 15 shots. The U.S. Department of Justice by the way considered that case when it issued a report that found the Cleveland Police Department engaged in a long running pattern.

Why out of all the races of people in the world, Blacks are singled out to be the worse and lazy people there are, but who was slaves in the country? Blacks. They were the ones in the cotton fields in the deep South. I have not read now where in history where Mexican was on any plantations or in slave. So why has it come from blacks won't work. I read where blacks had a hand in everything was built in this country. I never seen nowhere in a history book where a white man doing was standing up watching someone else work. So that let you know who are working even in the 1800s and 1900s. But he is quick to say I work hard for what I got. That's what they say down here in the deep South. But they got it wrong. Almost all the land whites own in the South was taken from the Indians and blacks. The ones that own it now don't even know how their parents and grandparents got it. They did not buy it. They stole people's claim long ago, so history say. If you got a spot of land first and stake a claim the land was yours. I know I read in books that some people murdered people down in the deep South and taken their land. You know the South has a lot to pay for. Slavery under paying the blacks murder. And they still murdering blacks in 2015.

I live in the deep South and it has always been a stumbling block. Blacks has always been underpaid in South Georgia but when you were born and raised in a place you would think that you can make it. And when you have children they would get a good job at home. Not so. I am retired. My dad had his own business here in the early 70s and 80s. Back then a lot of blacks had their businesses back then. But something changed in the 90s that made it hard for blacks to go to a bank and borrow money to start their business. So, the republicans came up with credit scores. When you live in the deep South you are being underpaid. You don't have good credit because you cannot hardly even eat, much less pay bills out of $7.25 per hour minimum wage for a family of four. Who can you pay? This is what put blacks in and below poverty. Then that is where food stamps, welfare comes in. So, you see what you have created by not paying people enough to take care of their family. I get so tired of hearing whites talking. Blacks need to go to work and stop living off the taxpayer. Guess what? The taxpayer need to pay them enough to support their family and they won't need their food stamps and all that goes with them. You see blacks have worked all their lives down here in the deep South. And now they want our children to work for their children for nothing. But guess what? What our kids are not going to do it. So, you have all the land and want all the money. So, work your farm. In a short time, the Mexican is going to see right what you are trying to do. Some of them have already caught on to what you guys on the farm are trying to do. Work them like you done the blacks from slavery up until now. To all the farmers in the deep South, you are going to pay up or get up and do your work yourself.

In the early 50s, we owned our own home, my dad and mom. We also had aunt and uncle and their little girl Chat. She was about three years old. Just tall enough to stand up and look out the back window of the car. We met a Jeep one of those back then. An army Jeep with about four white men in it. They were hollering and cursing. They were drinking. So, they seen we were black and man they turn around. You see, back in them days whites would pick at blacks. So my dad told my uncle they done turn around Charlie. And my uncle asked my dad did he his gun in the car? My dad said no. My dad I don't have anything in here but my car crank. But if they start anything, I am going to straighten this damn crank out upside their head. So, they drove right up behind dad's car and threw a full can of beer through the back glass. It spattered glass all in the baby's face and luckily no glass got in the baby's eyes. Dad pulled over and stopped. They went up the road and come back by calling us niggers. Dad told them if they stopped that Jeep he would show them how a nigger would beat the hell out of a white man. But them guys had done all they was going to do because they knowed if they stopped those two black men was going to beat the hell out of all four of them. You know back then white men would work with you all the week just as good. But when he gets with his buddies on weekend and start drinking he changed he be wanting to raise his foot like he going to kick you and call you names. That's just the way they were down here in the deep South back then. Blacks has always caught hell down South. They would work all week, six days a week from sun up till sun down for $15.00 a month. They called it run bill.

I am curious. By me being a black man, I often wonder do the white people ever have a conversation about blacks with their children. I told my kids about how blacks was brought over here to this country against their will by the white man as slaves. How they was in chains. And how they were auctioned off and sold like animals. Do you think the white man will tell his kids how we got over here? I know the question has been asked. But I would just like to know what he told his kids. You see I am not ashamed to sit down and talk about the past because we had done no wrong. You see we were done wrong. You see the white man cannot do that because he is the one that done everything wrong to the black race that could be done. So, you see he is not going to talk about blacks to his kids because if he does he will have to lie because he don't want his kids to know what his ancestors done to the black back in the day. But history will, and all the wrong doers will be uncovered. God will make it so plain till a blind man can see it. Even down in the deep South you people would walk up to a grown man and use the word (boy) and I think that was disrespecting a man. That went on for years down here. I can remember when I was about ten years old and a white man called my dad preacher. That made my dad so mad. Dad told him you ever heard me preach anywhere. The man said no. Dad told him "I am not a preacher. If you don't know my name, ask me and I will tell you." You don't give me a name. You can't call people anything just because you are white. Older black people in the deep South was not afraid of the Ku Klux Klan and the Klan knew this. Older blacks mean as hell back then. And they had guns like the Klan.

You know in 1865 congress passed what would become the civil rights act of 1866 guaranteeing citizenship without regard to race, color or previous condition of slavery or involuntary servitude. The bill also guaranteed equal benefits access to the law. A direct assault on the black codes passed by many Southern states. The black codes attempted to return ex-slaves to something like their former condition by among other things, restricting their movement, forcing them to enter into yearlong labor contracts, prohibiting them from owning firearms, and by preventing them from suing or testifying in court. The Civil Rights Act was vetoed by President Andrew Johnson, an uncompromising white supremacist. Congress overrode his veto in April 1866, but the experience encouraged them to seek constitutional guarantees of black's rights. In the deep South, blacks were able to vote in many areas but only through the intervention of the occupying Union army though the radical republicans had advocated legal equality between whites and blacks since before the war's end. From 1890 to 1910 poll taxes and literary tests were instituted across the deep South, effectively disenfranchising the great majority of blacks White only primary elections also served to reduce the influence of blacks in the political system along with increasing legal obstacles. Blacks were excluded from the political system by threats of violent reprisals by whites in the form of lunch mobs. And terrorist attacks by the Ku Klux Klan. Let's fast forward this 2015. The commander of Albany Sons of Confederate Veterans camp and another commander with the Sylvester based SCV camp say the flag does not represent hate and violence in the 60s. The Klan carried this same flag in Alabama during the civil rights movement. When the Klan was burning crosses and churches they were using the same flag. So why lie, the world seen it.

Ha, you know it. 2015 I would think the deep South would be better. It's not. You know I would look for the bad guys to commit murder. But not the guys that carry the badge. I wonder what country would let this keep on going on and the judge's call it justice. How can this be in America? The land of the free and home of the brave. Everybody taking about the Mexicans are murderers. And about them crossing the border. We already have murderers here who earn a pay check from the taxpayers. Then turn around and shoot their sons in the back or choke them to death or run them down with a car. Someone needs to step up and tell these judges to do something about all these white officers that is killing blacks. I wonder would the judges say its justified. I can tell you no, the judges that we have in the deep South is just as racist as they can be. Why would you want to have someone on a police officer who are a racist anyway? That gives the police department a bad name and makes the department a target to get sued. I am quite sure when they hire someone they give them a background check. They cannot tell if an officer is prejudice or not because if he is he will not tell you. Whites think blacks can't tell them they are prejudice, but they can. The way of blacks, whites will never know. Every black person is different. I have heard white people say all blacks are alike. That's a lie we all are not alike. That is why whites cannot teach black and won't admit it. They will keep sending the kid home saying they can't do anything with them. He won't learn nothing. No, you don't know how to teach him what he needs to learn.

6

Past Struggles

I just want to roll the time back and show the young people of this century what blacks had to go through to have a chance to vote. I did some research on how blacks in the deep South by 1910 most black voters in the deep South faced obstacles such as poll taxes, literacy tests, from which white voters were exempted by grandfather clauses a system of white only primaries and violent reprisals by groups such as the Ku Klux Klan also suppressed black participation. Every time the Klan terrorizes blacks back then and burn crosses they was carrying their heritage. But the white people of 2015 in the deep South say the Confederate flag does not represent hate. The Klan has never showed any love for the blacks. I would hate to see the hate. I am 77 years old and I have never heard or seen on TV where a Klanmans was shaking a black man's hand. There is nothing wrong with the flag. It's who you allow to use it and what they use it for. In the 20th century, the court interpreted the amendment more broadly striking down grandfather clauses in Guinn v. United States 1915 and dismantling the white primary system in the Texas Primary Cases 1927 – 1953 along with later measures such as the 24th amendment, which forbade poll taxes in federal elections and Harper v. Virginia State Board of elections 1966 which forbad poll taxes in state elections. These decisions significantly increased black participation in the American political system exempted white voters from a literacy test, finding it to be discriminatory. The court ruled in the related case Myers v. Anderson 1915 that the officials who enforced such a clause were liable for civil damages. I know blacks that vote today must be careful when they vote today, or whites will have you voting for the wrong party.

    I live in the deep South. You would think people would be changed more than they have. I was talking to some friends of mine and they said I have something to show you. I said let me see and he handed me the paper going to put this in it, so people can see how things were done in the 50s and 60s. The late Mr. Coes, Sr. was one of the first organizers of the Dooly County NAACP Chapter. He was also the one who instrumented in one distribution date for the surplus commodity program in Dooly when there were two distribution dates, one for whites and one for blacks. He was also an organizer of the voter registration on Drive in Dooly County, Georgia. The late Rev. J.F. Glover was the first black to attempt to vote in the City of Unadilla, Georgia, and was denied that privilege and afterward a cross was burned in his yard. Later he could vote and was the first black to vote in the City of Unadilla. The late Mr. Georgie Anderson was the first black to be appointed to the City Council in Unadilla. Mrs. Lucille Kendrick was the first black woman to run for a city council seat in Unadilla. The Rev. Charlie J. Anderson, Sr. was the first black to run for city council in Vienna, Georgia, but was not elected. He was told by some white people that he should be glad that he did not get elected because if he had he would have been killed. Mr. John W. Lester was the first black to be elected to the Vienna City Council and the late A. Bowen was next. Willie V. Davis was the first black to be elected mayor of Vienna after serving on the City Council. The late Roscoe C. Keaton was the first black to be elected to the Dooly County Georgia Road commissioners after a court ordered redistricting by the federal court. Mrs. Gail Bembery was the first black female to serve as city administrator for the City of Vienna, Georgia. Dr. Bobby G. West if the first black to be elected mayor in the city of Unadilla, Georgia. Mr. Emerson Lundy, Sr. was the second black man to be elected mayor of Vienna and Mr. Eddie Daniels is the third black man to be elected mayor of Vienna. There have been, and still is, many other blacks who have been appointed and elected to the political and appointed positions in Dooly County, Georgia, and including Pinehurst, Lilly, Dooly, Vienna and Unadilla, Georgia. So, what do this tell the whites? Blacks can run a city, but most of the time when blacks get elected in these small towns behind an outgoing white. They found money has been stolen and the city is in debt and the citizens don't know about it. So down here in the deep South, the whites has this good old boy system when they get caught with their hand in the cookie jar they just say Mr. John Doe retired or went to work somewhere else or he caught the first thing his picture is in the paper and on the TV, radio on the street and everywhere. They always try to put the black man down and what they don't know is that blacks are going to rise from under their feet. God has a hand on what is going on in this world. I may not be here to see it but the same people's that is being killed by the white man is God's people and when God lay his hands on these lying racist, judges and others who are lying he is going to show them up where their whole world can see who and what they has done to his people We blacks may not mean anything to the whites but we do to God and we are his children.

I have been looking on TV and reading about the Confederate flag issue. I don't see anything wrong with the flag itself, but what I have an issue with is when people try to cover up what it was used for. The older whites just like myself know what it was used for. The older whites just like myself know what it was used for in the 1800s and 50s and 60s so if it's your heritage put it in the museum. It's nothing wrong with that. But to march around from town to town is not good. The civil war is over, and the South lost so let's move on. I know we as blacks know what went on with the flag and try to teach our kids about the rebel flag, but we have a hard time teaching them at home when they white teaches at school are telling that nothing is wrong with rebel and the flag. I think the teachers know between but are a shamed of what their race done to the blacks back then. I know some or no why would people keep on marching with a flag if they are not trying to make a statement. You just don't march around with history. I don't believe this. They are not trying to make a statement. They are saying they do not march in black neighborhoods that is a lie. Because some blacks live white neighborhoods. You know what I think is going on here. Is the whites are trying to intimidate blacks that is not a good thing to do. But it's not rich white peoples doing this. It's the want to be rich and poor white that is doing this. You know when the civil war was getting on it was not all about slavery. The whites down here in the deep South did not want a government. They wanted things to stay like they were. Even today 2015, and whites don't want a government. I hear on TV we are going to take out country back. What do they mean? Are they talking about overthrowing the government? You would never hear blacks make a statement like that. It won't be like the civil war. So, you better think.

I have a question why the whites want a gun law to walk around with guns strapped on their side like they did in the old west. Who are they afraid of. This country supposed to be civilized. I don't get it. The blacks have guns. They don't want to walk around with guns on. I think if a man is that scared he needs to stay in the house. My dad used to tell me nobody tote a gun but a coward. I believe that you know I don't see any where a carrying a gun but down here in the deep South, Georgia. I know some of my people came down from up North and seen white man come in a store. They ask me if he was the law. I said no. He's just a farmer and he has a permit to carry it. My uncle said I don't care what he has he could not carry it in a store where I came from. I told him you are in the deep South he said I know. And I am ready to get the hell of here. He asked me why I was still here. He said your wife has passed away and mother and father. He said Cleve you and Amber need to leave this place. Don't let her get stuck here like you did. He said man you don't need to hang around a small place where white people are wearing guns like the 1800s. You know it is something is up when white people want laws passed down here in the deep South where they can have the same guns as the military has. You don't need those kinds of guns to hunt deer or anything. If you cannot hit a deer out of seven shots, you don't need a gun anyway. I seen this white man on TV in Savannah standing in front of an army recruiting office with a military rifle. Nobody told him to do that. Just because you are white. You cannot take the law in your hands. Guess what my cousin who lives over there say they told him he had to go, nobody authorized him to do that. He's gone.

 I know people raised in the South has always had problems most of all it is dangerous now that most Southern states has passed a gun law. Other states that not good. If a person is unable the person that issues don't know this when he issues the license. The gun law goes too far when they want guns in God's house and schools. When in some cases you have some whites don't like blacks. And he can carry a gun to school. Dad is going to help him get license to carry his gun because he has his. I know black dads are not going to let his son take a gun to church or school. The first thing a black dad would say hell no. Boy I will beat the hell out of you. You see us older blacks try to obey the law. But don't push the wrong button. What whites have a problem with they don't really understand the black race especially the black man. I don't think most whites think we are smart people, but they are 100 percent wrong. Just because we let them get away things they do to us. We know that they justice system do not work for us blacks. But one day before long the system will. Every law that were passed blacks had no hand in it. Especially down in the deep South. You know most all blacks that live down here knows how the system works. Just look. We had a black kid to be murdered and his body was found rolled up in a gym mat at Lions County, Georgia High School. The kid is black. Nobody knows who did it. Somebody did it, he did not kill himself. But if he had been white someone down here would have went to jail. With the kind of talk that has been going on. Someone knows who killed those people's son. I feel so sorry for them someone need to pay for this crime.

    I have a story to tell about a football team who calls themselves the Rebels. All the players are black. The blacks most all of them wants a mascot change but one white boy decided he wanted to play on the team. I wonder why. This team is in a small town about 176 miles south of Atlanta, Georgia. One white teacher put an article in our newspaper saying nothing is wrong with the team's mascot (Rebels) So what she said was she teaches her class. What I would like to say is why would you want to teach a class that nothing is wrong with a name that has held blacks enslaved and you have blacks in your class. Here is what I think the teacher don't know black history or her parents told her nothing is wrong with the name Rebel. I wonder did her parents or grandparents tell her the Confederate soldiers was called Johnny Reb. They were called Rebels so why would you tell black kids that its OK to be a rebel. The rebels were fighting the Union army who was fighting the South trying to free the blacks who were enslaved by the Rebels in the South. Mrs. School teacher you say Rebel is OK for a mostly black football team. You have to be sick or think blacks are crazy. Lady read some black history it will tell you all about Rebel. I think you know but think we don't know. If I had a kid in school and you would tell him nothing was wrong with Rebel. I would remove him from the school. The young blacks don't know about the name and what it has been used in. And for what. You can lie to them now but when they get out of your classroom they will find out you lied to them and what do you think they will think of you. I can tell you what they will say. That is a lying teacher.

    I think it is ridiculous for a school teacher to tell the kids in her class room that the word don't mean anything. When she has black kids in her class. The word Rebel goes with Confederacy. Because they were called Rebels. Look at history. It will tell you the South used Rebel. Just because a slim margin of blacks fought with the South does not make blacks rebels. And the Southern whites need to know that. OK, this is 2015 and we have a flag issue. The massacre in South Carolina where nine people were murdered by this monster and later he was seen on

TV with the Confederate flag. An afterward the governor of South Carolina ordered the flag to be removed from the state house. And that started a firestorm in the deep South. The whites started marching with the flag saying it does not represent hate or racist. That's a tough sell. It sure don't represent love for blacks. Tell the black race of people what it means. I can tell you what it means. Look why in the 40s, 50s, 60s, 70s, 80s and today every time the (Klan) have a rally or a march, they are carrying the Confederate flag or when they were burning crosses in black neighborhoods, so I don't mean trouble we for the black race from slavery. To lynching, murder, being burn alive. Ever since the Klan existed that flag has always been there when blacks were being brutalized and murdered. So, I don't know why the whites think the blacks should embrace a flag and a name Rebel that held them in slavery for hundreds of years. What the flag was used to let the South Confederate rebels, so you see that name helps represent all the bad things that has happened to blacks and now the whites are trying to brainwash the young blacks in school.

I am so tired every time I pick up a newspaper some white police officer has killed a black man. This is 2015 not the 1800s. Come on. You don't kill people because they break the law. You arrest them. I seen in the newspaper today, August 21, 2015, a young black man was killed by a St. Louis police officer August 20. Listen at what the officers said. Police identified the 18-year-old as Mansur Ball-Bey said he another African American were attempting to flee a home where police were executing a search warrant when Ball-Bey pointed a gun at the officers. Police said two officers then fired hitting him four times and killing him. They said drugs, stolen guns were found in the house. Some protesters expressed doubt over the police account of Ball-Bey pointing a gun. St. Louis police do not wear body cameras. But St. Louis police chief Sam Dotson said some officers videotaped the protests, during which shots were heard. You damn right when they shot him. Ferguson has been on edge since Michael Brown was killed on August 9, 2014. Browns' death was one of a series of police killings of unarmed black men and teens across the United States that sparked a newly movement under the Banner black lives matter. Listen the murder of unarmed black men and teens by white police officers has largely become a debate over how minorities are being treated. Has become a hot button politically and social issue in America. Republican senator and presidential candidate Marco Rubio on Thursday said the issues cannot be ignored. It's a reality in many communities in this country the relationship between minority agencies is terrible He told the Detroit economic club. Police need to do more to allow for peaceful protests rather than escalate them into violence. Said U.S.A. Senior campaigner Jamira Burley. Who was critical of St. Louis police actions taken Wednesday? Thank God somebody is watching these murders because their state laws isn't going to do anything to them.

I was at a city meeting and the person that was chairing the meeting was white. But he made the mistake and said you people and a lot of blacks were at the meeting. So, one black woman jumped up sand said what in the hell you mean? You people? I knew right when that this white speaker was in trouble. They think blacks don't know what that mean. But they do. They know that you are singling out a race of people but whites has a bad habit of that in the deep South. You would think in 2015 those kind of words and other words existed but they are very much alive down here. Maybe one day things will get better down here. I don't know whether the peoples will or not. But just like my dad used to say about moonshine whiskey. When the end of the world comes, a man will be standing with a gallon of moonshine whiskey. Try to make a point. Blacks will be here to the police offices that are killing blacks and unarmed blacks. You may kill blacks but can't kill us all more will come. You may have more guns than blacks, but you don't have enough to save yourself. Blacks were used by the union army in the civil war to get through the deep South's lines back in the war. You may call them stupid and crazy, but they are some of the smartest people in the world. Check black history. Whites really need to read black history then you will understand why black men act like they do to the white man in the deep South. So, remember the black man has a reason to act like he does. Do the white man? No, he would love the black man. All the black man has ever down here was plowed the fields work cheap. Don't forget what these whites did. Blacks were brought over here to work. That's what history say. Whites check black history then you will know.

I cannot believe the killings by the police officers in this country. Our leaders are worrying about stuff in other countries. Does black lives mean anything in America? When we have blacks fighting in the military to make it safe do blacks have to endure wit this injustice. Blacks suffered enough in the 50s, 60s. Is history trying to repeat itself? I hope not. Look questions surrounding police accounts of the shooting of a black teenager in St. Louis this week have prompted first calls for officers to be equipped with body cameras. I think the police department should be charged with Ball-Bey murder because they were ordered to put cameras on the officers after the Brown murder and they failed to do that and now another black teen has been killed. The officers say he pointed a gun. That's what the officers aid. The dead man can't talk. This is from wire reports August 22, 2015. It say when two white police officers fired four times at 18-year-old Mansur Ball-Bey Wednesday in a crime ridden part of St. Louis one bullet hit Ball-Bey in the back and struck his heart. Killing him almost instantly. Check this out. The police said he pointed a gun at them Now the victim has been shot in the back. Now watch this. He was able to run some distance after being shot. What I see is police lying there is not video and the police know this. I don't believe Ball-Bey had a gun. If he was pointing a gun, how he got shot in the back. What happened when he seen them they knew that he had stolen goods and drugs in the house and he was scared turn and ran they told him to stop and he did not, and they shot him in the back. The police think they can get away with this one like the other officer did. The federal government needs to step in and make these cities do what they are supposed to do if a police officer's commit a crime. He be punished just like anyone else. Can't do the time, don't do the crime.

    I do research on small to medium cities in the deep South to see how many blacks that are on the city board, school board and county commission board. I found in one city, Abbeville, Wilcox County, Georgia, which is 56 percent black and do not have any blacks on the city commission. It is ridiculous, its 2015 and whites still don't want blacks down in the deep South to have a voice in anything. I have been seething that still trying to be brought back that existence in the 60s. You have some black leaders died where blacks could vote. So please don't let their death be in vain. What we have to do down here is to watch these Southern governors in the deep South and don't let them bring that pole tax back in a different form. People may not know this it's still a lot of racism in the South. I think people who encourage it should be run out of this country. If the police in Sanford and witnesses had not lied George might would had got some time. I take that back because his dad is white and a judge. And Trayvon was a black teenager and that did not matter to them. I know one thing what goes around comes around. So, judge remember you has a son. Even though he's a murderer and I know you love him. I know the Martin family love Trayvon too. But one thing about the whole Trayvon Martin case everybody lost something. The Martins lost their son. And Judge Zimmerman you lost a son too. You know what court's injustice the court done was injustice. The world knows your dad both are going to stand before a just judge who will judge you for murder. Because you broke one of his commandments thou shalt not kill.

I read in the *Albany Herald* on August 25, 2015, that a group of whites called themselves red neck from Lee County went to Jacksonville, Florida, and did a march with the Confederate flag. Why would anybody in their right mind go out of state to march with a Confederate flag where a black teen has been murdered by a white man. They are trying to heal. They had their share of racial problems. I cannot believe the leaders of that city let that happen. Unless they want a lot of trouble. What you Georgia red necks need to do is stay in Georgia and don't go down in Florida and stir up trouble and run back to Georgia. People go down in Florida and stir up trouble and run back to Georgia. People all over this country know what that flag meant. It was used in the civil war by the South. The rebel troops used it and I am quite sure that blacks know what that flag represent. A Southern heritage festival is fine. But what with the flag? History needs to be put in a museum. You know the people in Florida some of them don't like to be reminded of what that flag was used for. One of the TV stations here was showing footage of our rally and in the middle of it they stopped and put in footage from a KKK rally. That's not what we're about at all. This is heritage festival we're having. I don't think the young whites know the meaning of this flag. If they did I don't they would love it so much. But you know some of them probably would because daddy said its ok. So, you are going to have speakers from the Sons of Confederate Veterans, voice of the patriots and league of the South organizations who with the elections coming up might give some insights that will be beneficial. I happen to believe the government we have today is not doing the American people a fair job. They're trying to turn blacks against whites making trade agreements that are hurting our country but focusing on heritage events like ours to district citizens. We're about history, not hate; they said. The government cannot turn blacks against whites. Whites can.

How can the government turn the blacks against the whites? The whites have never wanted a government anyway. That's some of what the civil war was about and slavery. What are they talking about whites enslave? The North fought to free them. You all fought to keep them in slave. And fought to try and overthrow the government. You cannot you'll wrong doing on the government. You see when you work blacks for nothing treat them like they are not human, murder them, and your law don't do anything about some white man or white police that kills blacks. That's when you don't have black friends. When you all sit on your hands and do nothing. And the judge and other officers in court knows. All these blacks that has been killed by these officers and nothing has been done. I wonder do you think black should love you? What you'll doing with that flag today is not getting you'll no points with the blacks because they already know the game you all trying to play. But today is not like yesteryear. I would just like to say it's not like the civil war days. Its 2015. You have more peoples of color than blacks. So, I would be more careful with that flag I would put it in the museum because I think you'll are getting on a lot of people's nerves. Because not only blacks are talking about it some of your people are talking about it too. So, if I was you, I would stop all these marches before things get out of hand. I wonder where the TV people got the KKK and put it in that footage you sure you did not have them in your march. You know when you have a big march people will just join in and you want even to know they are there.

 I wished someone would tell me what's going on down here in the deep South. We have whites marching all over the deep South with that Confederate flag. Is history trying to repeat itself? I hope not. People are trying to move on. That flag thing they are acting like children want to be seen when they make statements like this in the newspaper. My Southern heritage consists of mistreating of the American Indians and taking of their land and the slavery of African Americans for centuries many of the majority suppressed all the minorities' efforts to gain freedom and jobs, housing and education. It's ironic the majority is feeling like a minority while having lost nothing. This is what was in the *Albany Herald* Friday August 28, 2015. The ultimate hypocrite recently made claim that socialist liberal leftists are seeking to fundamentally change America and to destroy the constitution and the Bill of Rights. All of this was defining himself as a Confederate American for those who simply do not know. The Confederate Americans fired the first shot at the constitution and fought for the four years to support government of slavery and bigotry. It hurts to say this. Being conservative, but *Fox and Friends* has drifted into such silliness, like playing ball or beds outside or constantly cooking. When is all this racial unrest is going to end? I seen one August 28, 2015, in Baltimore I see in the newspaper that the officers are going on trial that are charged in the death of a black man. Baltimore has purchased riot gear. Why they have not purchased body cameras for the officers like they were ordered to do after the Brown murder? I could make more sense to purchase cameras before riot gear. It's like the police going got war with the citizens who are paying them to protect them. Freddy Gray, who died from an injury suffered in police custody, six officers have been charged in Gray's death. One with second degree murder and the others with lesser crimes are we going to ever see these police officers stop murdering our young black man? Somebody has to be punished. These judges has to do their job all these murders are not justified. I know they are not and the whole country know they are not. What we have is system that was created to fail African American people. So, it is a racist system. I don't care what anybody say. I still say it is blacks are never right. They are all ways wrong down here in the deep South. Are blacks going ever get any justice down here in the deep South? Today's young black men are walking targets for these coward white police officers in the South. Some of them wearing that badge don't even know that each one of those letters that spell badge stands for something. I would almost bet you most of them don't even know what the words are. I know every law department has bad apples in it. What you have to do is get them out. If not, you will have a rotten police department. What is happening down South, and whites has this good old boy system down here and they think they can do anything they want to you. That's why they don't want any government. The Fed's let each state set their rules. And when they elect one of them good old boy governors they friend or buddies you are going to have things going on in all your Southern states. Blacks being murdered by white police they know how the system is set up and they do these things they know they can get away with it.

 Justice department report on Ferguson unrest offers lessons in what not to do. The police respond to unrest in Ferguson, Missouri, last summer offers lessons in how not to handle mass demonstrations. According to a justice department report that warns such problems could happen in other places ruled by mistrust between law enforcement and the community.

The report flashes out a draft version made public in June creating a portrait of poor community police relations. Ineffective communication among the more than so law enforcement agencies that responded, police orders that infringed on first amendment rights and military style tactics that antagonized demonstrators.

The final version which is to be released on Thursday was obtained in advance by the Associated Press.

I don't think a police department need to learn from what happened in Ferguson. These white officers knew what they were doing. I think the whole police department should be taught a lesson. These guys just has been doing this for so long they just got laid back with it. But God has a way to stop man from doing unjust to his people. It is so sad. That Michael Brown had to lose his life for the cover to be pulled off the Ferguson police department. Lord don't let his dying be in vain.

I have never heard anything like these lies these white officers are saying. You know when they get caught they start lying. Police officers interviewed complained of inconsistent orders from commanders. With some saying there was no plain in place for arresting people or that they were unclear who they could arrest the whole Ferguson police department. Should be arrested from what I read about it. The Federal Government should be running these towns in the deep South. Trust me those officers knew what they were doing they were told what to do by their commander. They are lying to save the commander. Take them before a non-racist judge and they will tell the truth. The Ferguson shooting along with other deaths of blacks at the hands of white police officers sparked a national dialogue about police community relations and the role of race in policing. Several recent fatal shootings of officers including in Illinois and Texas have focused attention on violent crime and officer's safety. That is sad. But the bible says you going to reap just what you sow. It also says whosoever kill, shall be killed. That is one of God's commandments. Not mine. So that let us know don't be so quick to judge. All these black families love their sons. And all the police families love them. But it some difference between the two. Murders the blacks were unarmed and shot in the back by the police. The police had a chance. He had a gun. Michael Brown did not.

I am a Southerner. I was born in the deep South and I know how it was back in the days and I know how it is today. Some changes have been made and some has been made to look like it has been changed.

Ok, you see young black men are being killed today. They were being killed yesteryear too. The only difference today than yesteryear is the law is killing them today. Not like yesteryear when they were being lynched by mobs and KKK. This what one white wrote in one newspaper down here. I would like to see President Obama come out with a strong show of support for our nation's law enforcement officers. It is the right and responsible thing to do. That is all good. But what about those families that their sons have been shot in the back by these same officers. Give them national support for that? And he goes on to say people are being slaughtered simply because they wear a uniform and Obama is in Alaska renaming a mountain. I can tell you one thing about these good old boys down here when some of them get in trouble or being killed, they want the whole world to help even President Obama. I have never seen white people hate a man like these people down here. And they say that flag don't represent hate. They are right. They don't need a flag to hate. What does it take for whites to get along with blacks? I can tell you where they can start at. First, we both are men and we should be treated like men and respected as men. But the white men in the deep South has a problem with that. You have some want to do the right thing. But they have to slip and do it. But if his neighborhood found out he will tell his neighbor and the good guy is in more trouble than you. First, if you treat us like men and give the respect that you want given to you, then we can get along that is what keeping us a part. I never heard anyone down here in the deep South say the president need to do something about these white officers shooting these unarmed blacks in the back.

 I was just reading about some of the Ferguson reports and changes they say they made in the police department. A spokesman for the St. Louis city police department Schron Jackson said the agency had made multiple changes since last summer, including hiring more minority officers and launching a community engagement division. What our officers encountered during those first 17 days of unrest has forever changed policing Jackson said. We acknowledged such changes by the progressive steps on department has taken to build better community relationships. St. Louis county police chief Jon Belmar said demonstrations like the ones that occurred in Ferguson are unwieldly and difficult to manage by any precise measure and that law enforcement could learn from our successes and lessons learned. But he said the report provides only a limited snapshot. But why a limited of snapshots I think the police department has something to hide. Let's be fair here. A young black man has been killed. Let's put all the cards on the table here we are talking about a human being. When someone has been murdered you don't hold anything back whether it be a police officer or not. If he commits a crime, lock him up. I seen in the Dougherty County, Georgia, newspaper where one person was saying in what they call a squawk box of course Obama is silent on the police killings. These are the kind of remarks made down in the deep South by the good old boys. I seen so much hate in the eyes of the whites in the last few years than I have seen all my life. I don't know what is wrong down here backs have a right to be anywhere in this country just like anyone else. The whites may have all the guns down here. They think but they don't have enough to save themselves. One police die, and they want to lock up everyone. Police kill one black no one go to jail.

Studies shown down in the deep South that a large percentage of young black men are behind bars or under correctional supervision, putting fear and stereotypes quickly. They are all classified as criminals and yet such figures, scrutinized disclose a complex truth. Many young black men have sunk into the criminal justice system for a stark, surprising reason, the safety nets have disappeared. Many of these young black men failed by families, churches, schools. Indeed, by any source of nurture or discipline can be saved. Study after study expressed a shameful truth about the deep South. About one of every four young black men is in jail, prison or on probation or on parole in the deep South. But 47 percent of the prison population, the coalition for criminal justice put it plainly. It is accident that our correctional facilities are filled with African American and Latino youths out of all proportions … prisons are now the last stop along a continuum of injustice for these youth that literally starts before birth. In the deep South we have more than 40 percent of black children are growing up poor, mostly headed by women in some neighborhoods. They see few, if any, adult men going to work. The neighborhood houses and community centers that helped previous generations restless youth are gone or struggling. The police officers who once turned a delinquent kid or young adult over to a social worker don't do that anymore they take them straight to jail and to prison.

I am so glad it is getting cool down here in the deep South all this hot muggy weather will soon be gone. I hope things cool down here. We don't need any more murders down here special by the police or any law agency. And I hope the Confederate people that has been marching all over the South with their history. You know that same flag has been all over the South before now. I read about this same flag when I was going to school. I also know that the people that was carrying it back then was not for the love of blacks. I also know it's the same color now it was back then. Nothing has changed. Whites was carrying it back then and whites are carrying it today. Just different peoples. I know it did not represent love for blacks back in the 1800s and it don't represent love in 2015. Whites can say it don't represent hate all they want to, but blacks know better. I can remember hearing my great grandmother talking about the civil war with the North and South fighting I asked her grandma why they were fighting, and she said they was fighting to free the blacks who the South enslaved. The North was fighting to free them. And they did. And I ask my great grandma was she a slave? She said no baby, but my mother was. And she went on telling us about what her mother said about the nightriders better known as the KKK she said her mother told her how they rode horses and burned crosses in black people's yards, ride through black neighborhoods carrying a flag. I don't know why the whites are trying to sweep that under the rug what it represents. I don't care what anybody say that flag was carried in battle by the Confederate soldiers which was the South called Johnnie Rebel. The flag means something to whites. To blacks it mean hate.

Today is September 9, 2015. It is mostly cloudy down here. I can't hear anything in Georgia about the Confederate flag and I think the people are glad that the people made their point about the flag and the blacks hope it is over with for now. Peoples sometimes take things too far. But it's some more things that are talked about down here in the deep South. That's food stamps, welfare, whites down in the South have a problem with blacks who are receiving help from the government when they are the ones created the problem. If they would pay a decent wage where people could their family the government could do away with those programs. But until then, the government are going to take care of the poor. I know what it means to be poor. I have been poor all my life. But one thing about blacks we know how to survive. We can get our food out of the woods we are used to doing without. We are no stranger to hard times. We are used to not having enough money to pay our bills. We know what it feels like to be turned down at the banks for a loan. So, there is nothing much more can be done to the black race in the South. The only thing blocks can do down South is trust in God. He is going to lead us out of this just like Moses led his children out of the wilderness. We have been denied good paying jobs like the whites have even taught we can do the job as good as the whites. But it is what it is. It's even better for blacks in Florida than it is in Georgia and much better up North. That's why they leave Georgia.

7

Our Legacy

The public black high school of Turner County, Georgia, known as Eureka Elementary and High School of Ashburn which made its appearance in the early thirties. This school moved slowly for ten years or more. The class of 1941 was the first to graduate from the 11th grade with 16 units of work enabling its graduate to enter college. In the early years of Eureka, the following persons served as principal of the school. Mr. H.L. Williams, Mr. G.P. McKenny, Mr. E.E. Owns, Mrs. A.C. McKenzie. The homecoming activities that became a delightful part of our school days were in the 40s. In 1945, Mr. Hodge King became principal of Eureka and remained in this position until the integration of the Turner County Schools county-wide consolidation for high school students came in 1948 and the first bus for transportation was provided in 1949. Eureka made rapid progress in the 50s the first 12th grade class to graduate was in 1952, the football team was organized this same year with Mr. John Dye as coach. The school had 21 teachers on its faculty in 1953 an enrollment of 600 and four buses provided to transport students. The band was also formed in 1953 with Mr. Robert Cross as director. At this time the school owned a 46 passenger bus for transporting students on education tours and other trips connected with the school. In the fall of 1957 the students of Eureka entered the new school building. During this year, Eureka received its first free lunch program. The first yearbook printed for the school was the 1958 edition of the *Tiger*. Eureka continued to progress during the 60s as the school competed in interscholastic activities such as dramatics, debating, spelling chorus and orator contest.

The school was also well known for its football, basketball and track activities. The last days of Eureka as we knew it were during the 1969-70 school year. By this time Eureka had 40 teachers on the faculty and 1,000 students. The school was renamed for the 1970-71 school year. You see how whites treat blacks in the deep South. You see how they come in and take over all those years from the beginning. It was Eureka when the schools was integrated they came in and changed everything.

Mr. King was principal of Eureka. They made him assistant principal. They did away with our football program and mascot the Eureka Tigers. The program was organized by coach John Dye. They made him assistant coach for the Turner County Rebels. So, you see how they do down here in the dirty South. I wonder have they ever thought how they destroyed our school legacy. Not only in Turner County, Georgia, this was done in all Southern states. How can whites march around with a Confederate flag when they have destroyed all black schools and saved theirs when schools integrated what that flag does it's just as dangerous now as it was in the 1800s. No difference I know Eureka School was destroyed by a white school board and some more whites but that's fine. I know God has something in store for all these racist people in this world because they are not doing what they were put here to do. God has got tired of being lied to by his people. You were not put here to rob, steal and kill. That is why we are having all these storms and rains and out west they have all those fires that burn for months before they can put them out. God is trying to tell us to get out house in order because he is on his way back.

    I was talking with a friend who lives in Chatman County, Georgia, and he was telling me about the two police officers on trial for the murder of a black man at their jail. I just can't understand how we as peoples can sit on their hands and do nothing. Black lives do matter. All lives matter, how can our justice system let murderers get by just because they wear a badge. Therefore, the white officers in mostly Southern states are shooting blacks because the judges and the system are letting them get away with it. I bet if the system makes an example out of one of these white officers the killings will stop. You know everyone is talking about America and how it let blacks unarmed being murdered by its white police officers. I would just like to say if America don't change the only friend it's going to have is racist white people and black Uncle Toms. And that's no good for any country. You know when I was growing up in this country, I never thought I would see my black brothers shot down on the streets by our own police. When I grew up here back then the police would give you a ride home at night if you were a teenager not shoot you in the back and say they thought you had a gun. How long is God going to let this happen? It says whosoever kill. Shall be killed. That's not man's word. That's God's word. So, we can see his word are being fulfilled the law officers are being

    It is September 11, 2015. I buy a newspaper every day. It's a shame how the peoples down here make statements about these white officers saying everybody not just business, should show their support for officers through the back the blue program. All of us should put out a blue ribbon. That is good because we know that we have some good officers in every department. What we need to do down here is found out who the good old boys and racists and get them out of these departments and get them out and all these killings will stop. Bad as I hate to say this down in the deep South you have some whites that don't like black people and just can't make them like blacks. What the system must do is do away with those racist judges and racist district attorneys and then the system will work. We hate to see our officers get killed because of what some racist police has done that is why a race hater has no business wearing no kind of badge. But you read in these newspapers in the South where some racist whites say he should have done what the officers said. I live down here I have seen the white officers answer a call. They did not ask what the problem was or anything. They jump out of their cars with their hands on their gun cussing and calling niggers. We are going to lock your black asses up that is no way for an officer of the law to conduct him or herself. But that's the way they do it down here that's the way they do it down that is why we have so many blacks killed by the police. Do something there will be more blacks killed by the police. Because the police provoke it until someone do something there will be more blacks killed and more police killed. So, let us pray.

I can't help but sit and wonder why man wants to be over and control something he did not create. But some men think just because they are not, and they are white they are over you. Not so. God put man on this earth to be over the birds and animals and all the other creatures that he created. The white man down here in the deep South is just like me. All you white police officers and none police men in Phil 2:13-16, for it is God which worketh in you both to will and to do of his good pleasure. Do all things without murmurings and disputing that you may be blameless and harmless, the songs of God, without rebuke during a crooked and perverse nation, among whom ye shine as the lights in the world. Holding forth the of life; that I May rejoice in the day of Christ. That I have not run in vain neither labored in vain. Ye have heard that it was said by them of Old Times. Thou shalt not kill and whosoever shall kill, shall be in the danger of the judgment but I say unto you that whosoever shall say to his brother, Raca, shall be in danger of the council but whosoever shall say, though fool, shall be in danger of hell fire in Gal. 5:14 for all the laws is fulfilled in one word. Even in this thou shalt love they neighbor as thyself. It tells us in James 1:25 but whoso looketh in the perfect law of liberty and continue therein he being not a forgetful hearer, but a doer of the word, this man shall be blessed in his deed. So, you see God is telling us what will happen if we murder someone he don't care if you are a police officer that don't believe you the right to kill someone. But you see if you are black white police think that don't matter they think it's ok to kill blacks. That's the way they think here in the deep South. If you break God's laws, you suffer.

In the deep South, these are some of the things our young black men go through down here. The interaction our society has with young black men. This is not an excuse or even an explanation for any specific incident. It is just a context. Black males are in a long term economic and social explanation. But there most like interactions with public authority are a squad car or a demand for child support. These actions can't be the only outreach. What more can you do to the young black men. I can't hear anything from society about these young black men being shot in the back by white police officers. Where is society on this? Don't black lives matter in this country? Listen what this say. The main interaction our society has with young black men is merely criminal justice response to problems will ensure future resentment. Kindled into anger by future controversies a practical matter. White police officers in the deep South know what it takes to anger young black men. Thing like cussing, calling niggers and you don't have any businesses over here and much more. It's bad when you live in a country where society single out one race of people black young men must be the only one's live in this country that break the law. No, they are the only ones go to prison for crimes. Just in case society has forgot blacks were brought to this country against their will as slaves for this country by white slaves buyers and traders. Our young blacks don't know about black history. If they are not taught at home, because they don't teach the real black history the white teachers know our black history, but they don't want their kids to know what whites done to blacks back then but it's coming out.

I always love to read and do research for thing that happen in the deep South and I tell you a lot of things has happened down here. Here is something I ran across. Mary Turner an African American woman was lynched in Lowen County, Georgia. She was eight months pregnant. Her and her child were murdered after a public denounced the extra judicial killing of her husband by a mob. Her death is considered a stark example of racially motivated mob. It is sad to say in the deep South it is hard and dangerous for blacks to make it. I know lots of black families who are struggling trying to make it. Some homes don't have a man in the home. The woman is head of household. We have in the state of Georgia almost all your young black men are either in prison or locked up waiting to go to prison. I think its 85 percent or 90 percent young blacks that is locked up. Violence in the American deep South and was referenced by the NAACP Anti Lynching Campaign of the 1920-1930s. Mary is one of the 148 African Americans women who were lynched in America. I just had a thought run across my mind. You know all of us were born innocent. And you can be taught to love. A lot of people don't know who the author and creator of love is. It is God. So, if you hate your brother and say you love God, you are a lie and stand in danger of not seeing God's face because he only deals with love. I will tell you all my brothers out there if you hate your black brothers, you are going straight to hell.

    I see and read about this word justice all the time. It is *stunning what man* can do with a system that is supposed to be for all the people. But it is not. If you are black you will not get any justice in the deep South. Look at the Trayvon Martin case in Sanford, Florida. That was no justice and it did not start with the Martin case. It was no justice in the 1800s for blacks. Blacks have always been denied justice. It is a shame the way the Trayvon Martin case was tried in Sanford, Florida. The whole country was watching to see what the court was going to do with George Zimmerman. He had initially requested a hearing to claim immunity from prosecution under the stand your ground law. But this never happened making the law irrelevant to Saturday's verdict. But the torrent of criticism for the law that poured in from all corners of the nation has continued. The trial might be over for the jury, but it's not over with the Martin family and the blacks in Sanford, Florida. If George had been black and Trayvon had been white, what do you think would have happened? George would have gotten life in prison. No acquittal. No nothing but time. I know that Trayvon Martin will get justice. He did not get it in the courtroom, but I believe God will get it for the Martin family and no George you will get what's coming to you. Remember what the word says about thou shalt not kill. It also says whosoever kill shall be killed. If I was you George, I would be praying for your father can't save you in this case. Your father's friends or not the jury they are not the witnesses and they sure is not the judge. You alone have to give account at judgement day.

I know we as black race of people we take our faith in God and we do not joke around with Christianity. We are God fearing race of people. We do not play with God's word. I buy a newspaper every day and I ran across an article that Cal Thomas had written about Mrs. Davis had refused to marry a gay couple. By the way this was in the *Albany Herald*. And the name of his article was 2 Kingdoms in conflict over rights. I seen this. I got on the phone and call one my black brothers and told him about it and told him to buy a paper. I never read such in the paper he is talking about 2 Kingdoms. I had already known white people most of them are not Christian because if they were they would not kill and treat their black brothers the way they do. But they don't care. They know God is watching and still they break his commandments. We as black race of people we have to lean and depend on God. From which come our help. Our forefather's praise and depended on him when they were enslaved by these same non-Christian people down in the deep South. Any man that knew anything about God would not have wrote that in the newspaper. He is saying American is a nation in which Christians have a right to practice their beliefs in private. First, America is not a nation America is a country. You cannot enslave religious. The word says let your light shine. Why did the word tell us to work while it is day? Because no man can see at night. I am going to trust in the Lord most black people feel the same way that I do. You see I know who wake me up every morning. I know who my friend is. I am telling all my black brothers and sisters trust in God. Don't worry about those gay people, God will take care of it he did before, and he will do it again. I am not going mess with those gay people they are not going to take me to hell with them. I have enough hell down in the deep South with these devils down here. You know we have some white people down here think God is white. I work with a white man he told me God was white. I asked him how did he know? He said he seen his picture. I told him that was man made. No man has ever seen God. He looked at me like he was crazy.

I grew up in the deep South being black is real hard and dangerous. It is more dangerous now than it was when I was growing up. When my generation came along we did not have all those drugs like we have today. We had drugs cocaine, but poor blacks could not afford it. Only the rich whites, the only thing blacks could afford moonshine which was a cheap high. So, the only thing back then was a lot of work from sunup to sundown and know most of the whites say blacks won't work. That's the worse lie that was every told. Their parents have worked our parent for nothing all those years. But we are not going to work for nothing and that's why they say blacks won't work. I don't hear that anywhere but in this small town in Georgia in the deep South. In most of your small towns blacks are living below poverty and most of them cannot find a job so when you are living in small town USA it's hard. And now days the whites you thought was your friend are acting stupid because the blacks are talking about how these white police officers are killing these young black men for no reason and you don't know when one of them down here might do the same. Look what happened in our neighboring state Florida. Jacksonville, a young black man was.

    It is September 17, 2015, around 8:05 p.m. In the deep South in Georgia it is almost dark, and you don't need to be outside unless you have to. I notice down here where people have blue ribbons on their houses and cars. I asked one man what the celebration was. He said they was thinking law officers for what they do. I said that is real nice. I know we have some good officers on all law forces. I know we have some racist ones too. We have to come up with some way to identify the racist police officers. It sounds crazy, but we have to do something all these unnecessary killings and the courts are not doing anything about them. The judges and DAs don't care someone has to do something.

    It is September 18, 2015. I pick up my newspaper and begin to turn the pages and all of a sudden this pop up in front of my eyes. Virginia school suspends 20 over the Confederate flags. I said oh no not again. It's been weeks and I have not seen or heard anything about the flag. I don't have to tell you what color the kids are. I guess the flag don't mean anything, but their parents know. Students have to sign a contract agreeing not to display the flag to receive a school parking pass. WSLS TV in Roanoke quoted a Montgomery School spokesman as saying the Confederate flag was deemed offensive by school officials and that the suspensions were ordered as a result. The spokeswoman did not immediately respond to a request for comment. The way I see it the spokeswoman did not have anything to respond for the school has done that. I just would like to say the kids knew what the rules are, and they broke them. One thing about the whites down South, they think the rules are for the blacks and not for them. I can say blacks is not going to teach their kids anything wrong. If they know it's wrong. Because they know down here in the deep South if you favor someone down here that the law is looking for they will lock you up quick. Until they found the right one. It's hard and dangerous in the deep South if your skin if black.

    I get so tired of Southern whites talking about respect for people in authority. First, who are in the authority have to give respect too. Just because a person is of that don't mean you can disrespect them. That's why blacks in the South have problems with whites in the deep South. You never grow up. It's that H"a-boy thing. You can be 50 or 60. It's that h"a-boy thing we as black men want to be respected as men just like any other man. Listen at this. There would be no need for more law to correct sagging pants. Is that why police departments hire more officers. I got this out of our little paper down South. So, you see how these people think down here. The president has authority. No one ever has respected him but the blacks. Whites has never respected him or liked him. Not even congress listens at this. Shocking to many Americans to see the violent reactions of Southern whites to the efforts of the blacks to win the right to be respected as a customer in places of public accommodation. This was won in the 60s. How easy do people forget. Especially our white brothers. I am going to share something with you that happened in the 60s. Because I know some of you was not born the die-hard white people in the South are losing in this fight, not only for themselves, but for their states and region. While striking at us in the name of a dead past, they are hurting their region and their country. In today's changing and threatening world our government system is on trial. Is this the land of the free or only the land of the white free? If it is the latter, then we should prepare to join South Africa at the bottom of the list of nations for there is no place to prestige or power in the world of the 60s or 70s for a Jim Crow Nation. For the first time since reconstruction, the black condition in America was central issue before the American people. Unlike any previous age the drama unfolded in every home. All America had demonstrators singing "we shall overcome" There was a sense of pride and determination in the black participants that compelled respect, if not sympathy.

    I am going to share something our young peoples that most of them don't even know about and some was not even born. What we seen the last two or three years about our young blacks being murdered by white police officers it did not just start it has been happening. It has always happened in the deep South during civil rights movement in the 60s. In June 1963, Mississippi Field, Secretary Medgar Evers was gunned down in front of his home. The nation was shocked, and protestors poured into Washington, DC, demanding Federal action on civil rights. As the funeral services for Medgar Evers held in Jackson's Masonic Hall, Roy Wilkins delivered the following eulogy: "There have been martyrs throughout history in every land and people in many high causes, we are today in tribute to a martyr in the crusade for human liberty. A man struck down in mean and cowardly fashion by a bullet in the back." Many blacks suffered back then and was killed by police and white citizens. So, the killing of black did not just start in 2001 and on. The climate in Black America in the early 60s is difficult to describe. The masses of black people were involving themselves in the struggle for the first time. The student movement of the South sparked a wave of political agitation unknown in American history.

It's a beautiful day down here in the deep South. The sun is shining beautiful this 20th day of September 2015. The breezes are blowing through the pines in Georgia. You can smell that Southern chicken cooking to a golden brown. The pecans begin to open, and you can tell fall is not far away. Everything is quite down on this end, but you could wake up next morning and somebody tell you something bad happened last night. We as blacks have to be real careful. Me and two guys were talking the other day how strange the whites are acting down here. I said man I don't know what is wrong with them. In South Georgia is worse than North Georgia. Being black you know some whites look at you like it's a sin. Let's back up. The climate in black America in the early 60s is difficult to describe. The masses of black people were involving themselves in the struggle for the first time. The student movement of the South sparked wave of political agitation unknown in the American history. In Philadelphia attorney Cecil B. Moore became branch president and led thousands of demonstrators at construction sites where no blacks were employed despite the involvement of public funds. Mr. Moore was an extremely plain spokesman who rallied support for the association among poor blacks in North Philadelphia. Southern branches such as Savannah, Georgia, NAACP branch under the leadership of W. W. Law brought the downtown merchants to their knees with a boycott demanding employment. You know we have stuff going on today would have went on in the 60s. The young blacks are too hard headed to listen to the older blacks. Until they listen, we older ones could tell them how to stop all the stuff that his happening to them. Because we been there. We know how and what to do to stop it.

I am going to tell you a story about myself when I was living in North Georgia for about two years and I came back down here to visit my parents. I was never intent to stay here because even then I could see this place was not for people of color. I see it back then. I can see the same thing now that I seen 50 years ago. That is poor blacks living below poverty and unemployed. Those that are employed are being low wages not enough to get by and then you wonder why they are selling drugs. You drove them to breaking the law by not paying them enough for working to take care of their family. You put them on food stamps. You put them on Medicare and Medicaid. Mr. White man you are to blame for everything that happens to blacks in the 1800s to 2000s. You have always robbed the black man even today you are trying to kill all the young men. Today 2015 blacks are still being locked up because we have racist judges sitting on the bench. The prison in the deep South are 95 percent black and people of other color. America this is not what Dr. King gave his life for and I know he is not happy the blacks are not standing up for what they should be. We are treated in a way worse than the 60s in 2015. The young blacks will not stand up like us older blacks stood in the 60s. We was ready for anything that came our way. I can remember some of us went to jail and some went to the hospital, but we did not care. We still stood for what was right. I can tell you today I am an old man now and I will still stand for what is right. I might not can stand as long as I used to, but I will stand. My dad always told me if you are right stand on it. If you have to stand by yourself do it. If God is with you the devil in hell cannot harm you. I have always told my two daughters this stand for what is right and you will be ok. In my life I have been in places where people did not like me because the color of my skin. But we did not make ourselves so if people going to dislike someone because of skin color you know what? They should ask the one that made all these pretty colors and get on their knees and pray for forgiveness.

It's a hard life in the deep South for unwed young black mothers. Most of their kid's dads are in jail or on their way to prison. The system will not give our young black males a chance. I know some young men went to prison because they would not tell the police someone's name. When you put the father of the kids these young mother's have you are creating a problem. The state has to take care of dad and his kids then that's when black mothers go to welfare and food stamps. All because dad did not tell the officer what he wanted to hear. Or he caught him with a little marijuana problem enough to make one cigarette. Then he goes to jail and before one of those good old boy judges and he gives him five to 10 years in prison. Ok when he gets out of prison no one wants to hire him because the judge took a misdemeanor and made a felony out of it. And you know what that means down here. No one will hire him and that's another problem he can't get a job. Ok let's stop here. This is what the justice system does to young black men. It sends them to prison for almost nothing for if they were white they probably would not go to jail little lone prison down here. Then the whites down in the deep South say that young blacks won't work, that's a lie. The white mans' justice system down here has their life screwed up so bad with the work laws nobody has but them won't let them work and right back to prison so how the system work down here for young black men.

    I would just like to share with you how powerful the NAACP was in the 60s and how weak justice is today. The perceptions of Americans as to who they are required after much agony and hesitation, the decision to bury segregation as was required by Southern laws. The NAACP has led the way with its lawsuits and subsequently with demonstrations and voter registration naming all the heroes and heroines of this struggle is not possible nor is it possible to exaggerate the central role of the NAACP in the creation of the new South. The peak of the 60s movement for full equality for Americans of African descent was reached in 1963. The whole of the country was locked in struggle. North and South, East and West. NAACP branches and youth councils were challenging the established order and demanding redress of ancient grievances. The movement has seen some success. In 1962, President Kennedy had ordered the federal housing authorities to cease discrimination related to the financing of private home construction. The young president also appointed black people to visible positions of power and influence in the federal government. Dr. Robert Weaver, chairman of the NAACP national board was appointed administrator of the federal housing and home finance agency. The highest position ever held by a black man in the federal government. Kennedy had won election due to strong support from black democratic voters. He was under tremendous pressure to demonstrate that he deserved that support. You watch a democratic president that do a lot for the black race of people. He either get voted out or murdered. Kennedy had also moved forcefully in the integration of University of Mississippi in 1962 James H. Meredith had been admitted to the school on September 30, but it required United States' marshals and federal groups to insure Meredith's safety. The NAACP experienced dramatic growth during the years and its income also soared. Despite the attacks on it from those who regarded themselves as more "militant" the association was respected for its reliable and steady leadership in the equality and justice. More NAACP branches and youth councils were chartered and in every part of the country the association was not merely in the think of the struggle, it was often, in the leadership of it. You know what? We have got to get our NAACP branches all over the country back like they was in the 60s and we can all these police killings of our young black men. We has got to go back to the old landmark and make them respect this organization today like they did in the 60s we have to do what we have to. We have no time to waste. It has to be done quickly.

In the 60s black Americans was everywhere demanding change the way blacks were treated, and the police were violating black's civil rights. We did not ask, we demanded it. White America was near a state of shock with all these demands. This is what our young blacks have to do. You will never get anywhere asking. You have to demand. What happened in the 60s will work today. You just have to have a plan and know how to use it. There are some things us older blacks can teach you young men if you guys would take the time and listen. We are not going to tell you to hurt anyone and not hurt yourself either. We are having struggles now just like we had in the 60s. It's began to look almost like the 60s all over but I hope not. You see we had murders in the early 50s. We had a teenager murdered in Mississippi by the name of Emmitt Louis Till was killed August 28, 1955. He was only 14 years sold after reportedly flirting with a white woman. How can a 14-year-old flirt with a grown woman? Twenty-one-year-old Carolyn Bryant who is white lied on this kid; anyone read the story know what went down. Her husband Roy and his half-brother J.W. Milam killed this kid. Now the people they are doing today the only difference now the people that's doing it today are wearing a badge. What do that tell you? If police officers had been doing this in the 60s, the NAACP would have gotten someone's attention with lawsuits. These cities need to be held accountable for these officers.

Till was from Chicago, Illinois, visiting his relatives in Money, Mississippi, in the Mississippi Delta Region when he spoke to 21-year-old Carolyn Bryant the married proprietor of a small grocery store there several nights later Bryant's husband Roy and his half-brother J.W. Milam went to Till's great uncle's house. They took Till away to a barn where they beat him and gouged out one of his eyes before shooting him through the head and disposing of his body in the Tallahatchie River weighing it with a 70-pound (32 KG) cotton gin fan tied around his neck with barbed wire. Three days later Till's body was discovered and retrieved from the river. Till's body was returned to Chicago. His mother who had raised him mostly by herself insisted on a public funeral service with an open casket to show the world the brutality of the killing. The open coffin funeral held by Mamie Till-Bradley exposed the world to more than her son, Emmitt Till's bloated mutilated body. Her decision focused attention not only on American racism and the barbarism of lynching but also on the limitations and vulnerabilities of Americans.

Tens of thousands attended his funeral and viewed his casket and images of his mutilated body were published in black oriented magazines and newspapers rallying popular black support and white sympathy across the U.S. Intense scrutiny was brought to bear on the condition of black civil rights in Mississippi. With newspapers around the county critical of the state, although initially local newspapers and law enforcement officials decried the violence against Till and called for justice. They soon began responding to national criticism by defending Mississippians which eventually transformed into support for the killers. In September 1955, Bryant and Milam were acquitted of Till's kidnapping and murder protected against double jeopardy. Bryant and Milam publicly admitted in the interview with *Look Magazine* that they killed Till. Problems identifying Till affected the trial partially leading to Bryant's and Milam's acquittals and the case was officially reopened by the United States Department of Justice in 2004 as part of the investigation. The body was exhumed and autopsied resulting in positive identification. He was buried in a new casket which is standard practice in cases of body exhumation. His original casket was donated to the Smithsonian Institution.

8

Murders in the Deep South

In the deep South we have a lot of unsolved murders. I know several such cases in a small town down South call Turner County, Georgia. In can't remember the exact date but it was in the 80s when an inmate they said by the name of Louise Holley committed suicide. But none of the black people believed it then and they don't believe it now. This is what the law said happened. An inmate was found dead in her cell Tuesday night at the Ashburn jail according to Turner County Sheriff Lamar Whiddon. Louise Holly, 32 of Ashburn was found dead in her isolated cell by a police officer approximately 8:30 p.m. Whiddon said. Holly was a Turner County prisoner that was held at the city jail. Because of overcrowding at the county jail, Holly had attempted to hang herself at the jail before, but jailers discovered her and stopped the suicide attempt. Whiddon said Holly had been convicted of forgery and was sentenced to three years in the State prison. She was awaiting transfer to the state penitentiary at the time of her death. The 38-year-old had been in jail before for shoplifting and other misdemeanor charges and had problems with other inmates at the jail. Jailers had removed sheets and the mattress from the cell for fear that Holly would use them to take her own life. Holly was moved to the isolation cell to prevent altercations with other inmates and for her own protection. Whiddon said the exact time and cause of death have not been determined but the body has been sent to the Georgia crime lab in Atlanta for an autopsy. It appeared the woman suffocated on a piece of plastic. Whiddon said some time later someone told the family some years later a police officer was suspended because of the suicide happened on his shift but they did not name anyone. But the acquisition then and still is how this black woman was in an isolated cell with no sheets or even a mattress in the cell. How did she suffocate herself with a plastic bag over her head? I was working at the hospital at the time when this happened. So, I asked one of the doctors could someone suffocate themselves with a plastic bag over her head? He said no, he said because you will pass out then your hands will fall off the bag and you will get some air. He said he has been a doctor a long time and he never heard that lie before. He said the only that could have happened someone held her down and suffocated her. Most of the family did not buy that. Mr. Holly told me and my dad that he knew someone killed his daughter and he was going to find out who it was. It's a lot of murder cases in Turner County, Georgia, has not been solved. A murder case is never closed until you catch the murderer.

    I worry a lot about myself and my family being black and living in the deep South where you know you are hated by a race of people for what you have never done no one in this country any harm unless it's because you are black. I read somewhere Oscar Hemmerstein wrote you got to be taught to hate. One can also be taught to love. Dr. King once said you need to know darkness cannot drive out darkness. Only light can do that. Hate cannot drive out darkness. Only light can do that. Hate cannot drive out hate. Only love can do that. So, to all you haters out there, remember God also say he is all about love. What are you going to say he is all about love what are you going to say when you meet our father who are in heaven that you hated your black brothers. You see we as a black race of people we fear God we praise him. Out of all our white brothers has done to us God still say we are supposed to love our brother. You know we were all born innocent people. We as a race of blacks we talked about more than any race in this country. We be denied good paying jobs in this country instead of being 100 percent we have to be 150 percent to come closest to being paid what our white brother is paid. No matter what kind of degree you have, especially in the deep South. I seen a lot happen down here. The only degree you will need down here is being white. If you are white you are right. If you are black you have to stay back. So, you see we are never given a chance down here.

    It is October 1, 2015, in the deep South and the weather is mild and looks like we might get some rain down here. But other than that, it is business as usual. Blacks down here are still jobless down here in this small Southern town. You have a few jobs but not many jobs are coming. We have a nice young lady at the Chamber of Commerce that is working hard to get this town on its feet and get jobs back here, but I don't see anyone else trying to help her and that by itself makes me wonder. If it was a younger man I would be right by her side asking her what did she want me to do. I don't see anyone doing this. So, what do that tell you. They don't want anything here. They want the town to stay like it is. That is why a lot of black families are moving away. There is nothing for blacks to do here but work to these few fast food places that are here and they don't pay enough to take care of a family. By the way they split 40 hours between three or four workers. These kinds of jobs that put poor blacks below poverty and put them on welfare and food stamps. And then you can hear whites say blacks won't work. That is not the case. Blacks will work. But they want to get paid enough to take care of their family just like the white man then you all can keep your food stamps and welfare and give it to the older peoples and the disabled and everyone will be happy.

Ashburn family wants truth about Greg's death. I never believed it was a drowning since the beginning. I believe it's a murder. The family of a man whose body was found in a Turner County, Georgia pond in March is holding a rally Sunday to make sure that Greg Wallace's death remains remembered in Turner County, Georgia. Wallace went missing March 14, 2005, and his car was found later beside U.S. Highway 41 South. Five days later, his body was found floating in a nearby pond. After months of investigation Turner County officials announced in June Wallace probably drowned and that there is no indication of foul play. Listen at the official's announcement. Probably meaning they don't know for sure. However, the Wallace family remains unconvinced. During the days that Wallace was missing, the family contacted Lynn Ann Maker, a psychometrist from Cedar Rapids, Iowa. A psychometrist is a person who reads psychic impressions from objects or locations, although law enforcement officers searched for days looking for Wallace with dogs and helicopters. It was Maker who found him. She was walking around a pond when his body came floating to the surface. Maker talked with the Wallace family and used her talents to perform a psychic reading on the mysterious death. Combined with their own suspicions, the reading led the Wallaces to believe that the death was more than a probable drowning. This is a death in Turner County that someone here knows about. And pay for it one day.

I would just like to share something with you about something happened in this small town. In the deep South Ashburn Turner County, Georgia in March I heard that someone was missing. But did not pay too much attention to it until someone called my house and said your cousin is missing. So, I got in my car and went where everyone else was down state route 41 where a lot of kin peoples was at the pond beside Highway 41. So, we went everywhere looking for Greg that night. It was so cold that night I think someone had moved his car. They said his car had been on the side of the highway for a day or two. This was in March 2005. The next day we looked at the pond he was not in it. So here is what happened. This psychic Lynn Ann Maker put up a website offering free reading. In early March just, last week she got an instant message from the Greg Wallace family in Turner County. Then she had a dream about Greg Wallace. So, she gathered her crew and drove 17 hours from Iowa to Ashburn. The next day we went and told my secretary and friend, and I said I know he's passed on. I know he's underwater said Maker. She says she need a personal item from Greg which his cousin Marc provided. Before I asked them to get together some stuff up for me, like I needed something of his unwashed and they gave me his jersey said Maker. Saturday, they drove to the area where Wallace's car was found along state Route 41 where investigators initially searched. They worked very hard.

In trying to find him. They worked up lead, they did an awesome job said Maker. Lynn says she kept feeling that Wallace was submerged in the water. I saw trees, but I was looking up and to me I was trying to make sense of it. What it was, he was submerged in water and he was under the looking out at the trees, and I was him. You know, in his body. The group checked other locations and why family members and others checked other locations in Turner County because we were told by law officers that they had searched the pond. If they and searched the pond, and did not find his body, where was it? And how it got back in the pond. But Lynn kept being pulled toward the pond. The group went to the right. But Lynn said there was something telling her to go left. So, I went around the tree. I was kind of looking towards where I was getting pulled. Behind some bushes, right there, he came up said Maker. Greg Wallace's body floated to the surface right in front of her. See part of his ear and the back of his neck, Said Maker. All of us family members know this was no mystery, it was a murder. No one was caught or charged. If a man drowned he will have water in his body. But if he is killed and put in water he will not have any water in him because he cannot suck in water. I heard one time they were talking about a dry drowning so asked a doctor at Tifton about dry drowning he said no such thing. He said that young man was dead when he was put in the water.

In 2005, the Wallace family recently contacted another psychic medium, John Maronge, of Pennsylvania who has helped the family investigate the death by unconventional means. Maronge said that as a medium he makes contact with the spirits of the deceased to provide closure to their family members. I communicate with the people who has passed on, he said. My readings usually consist of me not knowing much about the person. I am ready for. I was contacted by the family of Greg Wallace because there's some mystery surrounding the demise, so I am seeing if I can fit some pieces in. It's about time these people got a voice, Maronge said. That he performed a reading for the Wallace family but would not reveal the content of that reading. Saying that he keeps his revelations confidential to the victim's mother. Geraldine Wallace said that she did not want to talk about his reading because she could not prove what he said, and she might be in jeopardy of slandering another person she believes killed her son. Wallace did say that Maronge's reading was very similar to the psychic impressions expressed by Maker and that his readings filled in many of the details left out by the psychics. When asked if based on the information given by the psychics if she thought her son's death was a drowning, Wallace said that she thinks foul play was involved. It was never a drowning it was a murder. That's right. Mrs. Wallace. It might be 50 years, but someone will pay.

I thought the so-called drowning of Greg Wallace should be told. I got permission from his mother Mrs. Wallace. She still says today she never believed it was not a drowning, it was a murder, but you will have to prove it. Now Maronge has been visiting with the family for a week to help organize a rally Sunday at 3:00 p.m. at the Ashburn youth recreation park on Martin Luther King Jr. Drive. The rally will include a speech by Mrs. Wallace and possibly others whose family members have been victims of unsolved deaths in this small town which is 65 percent black in the city of Ashburn, Turner County, Georgia. Even it has been 10 years, and no one has been punished for it most all blacks in Ashburn believe it was not a drowning but a murder. So, I guess the case is still open. I think a murder case stays open until solved. A rally will be held to help the Wallace family raise money for an attorney and Maronge has offered one of his readings as an award. He usually charges $300 per reading. Hot dogs and hamburgers will also be sold. Wallace said that she hopes the rally will bring the community together and keep the death of her son in the minds of the public. She said she hopes that it will resolve some issues and shine some light on some of Turner County's unsolved murders. I hope something comes out of it. Wallace said at least there will be some attention. I have heard that Turner County was being watched because of all these unsolved murders and nobody going to jail but blacks.

The Rosewood Massacre in Florida, have you ever heard of the Rosewood Massacre? A violent racially motivated conflict that took place during the first week of Rosewood was abandoned and destroyed in what contemporary news reports characterized as a race riot. Racial disturbances were common during the early 20th century in the United States reflecting the nations rapid social changes. I am glad what I am about to tell you what happened in Florida, did not happen where I grew up. The state of Florida had an especially high number of lynching's in the year before the massacre including the well-publicized Perry race riot where a black man had been burned at the stake in December 22. Who would do a human being like that? I so glad things has gotten better. But still they are not where they need to be. We as black people still has a long way to go. The struggle is not over by a long shot. The town of Rosewood was a quiet primarily black, self-sufficient whistle stop on the seaboard airline railway. It is believed that this massacre of many black lives was spurred by unsupported accusations that a white woman in nearby Sumner had been beaten and possibly raped by a black drifter from nearby towns liked Rosewood. They don't know whether the man they lynched did the crime, they just got the first black man they saw. Just like today they say all of us is just alike and that is a lie, we all are not just alike. That's how mistakes are made with us. When black citizens defended themselves against further attack. Several hundred whites combed the countryside hunting for black people and burned almost every structure in Rosewood. I wonder do we have people like that where I grew up. No, we don't have anyone in Ashburn that come close to doing what those people in Rosewood done. Survivors hid for several days in nearby swamps and were evacuated by train and car to larger towns. Although state and local authorities were aware of the violence, they made no arrests for these murders in Rosewood. Are we living in Rosewood? The town was abandoned by black residents during the attacks. None ever return. Although the rioting was widely reported around the country few official records documented the vent. Survivors, their descendants and the perpetrators remained silent about Rosewood for decades. Sixty years after the rioting, the story of Rosewood was revived in major media when several journalists covered it in the early 1980s. Survivors and their descendants organized to sue the state for having failed to protect them. In 1993, the Florida government body commissioned a report on the events because of the findings Florida became the first U.S. State to compensate survivors and their descendants for damages incurred because of racial violence. I thank God that none of my people or friends people were in that part of Florida at that time. I also want to thank God that I live in Georgia because Florida don't do anything to murderers. See what happen with those murders in Rosewood. Nothing.

This might not be the place to put this but as a writer I just cannot look over all the killings going on this country for the past months of September on into October 2015. This country made a bad mistake to pass a gun bill like this. Nobody to blame but this congress. Now I need to ask a question. Is America a Christian country? All that is happened here makes you wonder. I was already troubled about a recent commentary that I ready last year about this country's Christianity. You see all the trouble that goes on here, people in other countries are seeing how our government let the judicial system break laws it created. It confirmed that America is a Christian nation by tolerating religious criticisms. That is turning the other cheek. Luke 6:29. There are non-Christian nations in the world where insulting religion could warrant death or imprisonment. The author tried to discredit Christianity by listing human shortcomings, but she highlighted the magnificence of Christianity. All humans have fallen short of the grace of God. Thankfully God is merciful. God so loved the world that he gave his only son that whosoever believe in him shall not perish but have eternal life John 3:16. That is the reason for the season and the reason for our hope and joy. I agree the pilgrims did not found America but if one read the writing of the men who did found the United States. It is evidence they were deeply religious. Not only in their personal writing but God is referred to several times in the Declaration of Independence. They believed God is the source of our liberties and providence every constitution makes reference to God. Our presidents are sworn in with hand on the Bible to indicate their recognition of the ultimate authority. Few people are aware of that following George Washington's inauguration he led the first senate and house representatives to St. Paul's Chapel to pray, most likely for God's guidance over our country. The United States is not a theocracy. The ten commandments is on the face of the Supreme Court building. Christianity teaches repentance and forgiveness. Similar to the working of our judicial system. Those who stop their illegal sinful behavior after making amends are forgiven. Just a Christ who said to a sinner, go and sin no more. John 8:11. Contrary to what was stated in what I read. The concept of equal rights and freedom for all is a biblical in origin. There is neither Jew nor Gentile neither slave nor free. Nor is there male and female. For you all are one in Christ Jesus. Galatians 3:28. This was the initial teaching that led to freedom and equality for all. Many times, America has sent its young men and women to war to protect others from being oppressive nations and tyranny of some non-Christian regimes. Not to conquer but to free people in the U.S. are being oppressed and killed every day and nothing is being done. The judicial system does not work for people of color. Our system needs to fix. We are having too many killings of our young people in our schools in this country. I am a senior citizen and I have never seen those many killings in school before in my life. That gives our country a black eye and we don't need any more. And most all the murders are being done in the Southern states and the deep South. What is wrong? I should have asked that you know why? Because everything that's going on today is in your Bible. It tells of all these things we just have not been reading it. All this stuff has to happen because the Bible said so. What the word said. Before my word fails heaven and earth will pass away. Look what happens families are killing one another Men want to be women all this sin.

It's November 2015 and police officers are still shooting unarmed black men in the back. Somebody please tell me when this will stop. Another black man was killed on Sunday, November 15, 2015. He was unarmed and shot in the back by a Minneapolis, Minnesota, police officer. Jamar Clark, 24, died on Monday night November 16, 2015 after his family decided to disconnect life support. It is a shame that this country will not put a stop to these coward police officers from keeping on shooting our young black unarmed men in the back. The young man was murdered, and the officials has already confirmed that no weapon was found at the scene. Now I just want to see what unfold next. Why were the young man running to see what the young man was running from in the first place? They say that are looking into whether Clark was handcuffed. They are saying that the police union said Clark grabbed one of the officer's guns. Although the weapon remained in its holster. I see right now what they are trying to do in Minneapolis they are going to try and cover the officers. But a good attorney will blow that case away. Why they don't want anyone to see the video? Because it is going to show what happened and the officials know it's going to show the truth. Mr. Brooks' president of the NAACP are pursuing them to see who videos they are going to have to let them look at them or its other steps Mr. Brooks can take, and they will be glad to let them see them. He was shot two blocks from the 4th Police Precinct station. Two officers have been identified.

It is November 19, 2015, down in the deep South. Something is always happening down here. Not a big deal. You have people down here trying to take nothing and make something out of it. Albany State University was once an all-black school. But it is not now. The board of Regents are merging Darton College with A.S.U. and the whites are going nuts. But if A.S.U. was merged with Darton you would not hear anything from them. But any time they do not get their way, they squawk. But they have to understand Albany State's legacy as a black college while important from a historical perspective, is no longer relevant in a global educational community and Darton's reputation as a two-year white alternative is not even valid any more. This is why the whites are showing their racist colors. We as blacks should be angry, but we are not. But time moves forward, and it has a way of dragging even the most stubborn of us along. When it comes to consolidating two institution of higher learning it would be heard to find a more oil and water mix. Albany state is one of the country's few remaining historically black colleges and universities designated institutions, a small undergrad liberal arts school established more than a century ago as a place where blacks denied the opportunity to attend other Southern colleges could further their education and pass it on to others of their race. You people in the deep South really show your racist side in Albany, Georgia about Albany state and Darton thing. If everything goes your way, we'll vote Republican. If everything goes your way, we'll do what you tell us to do, act the way you want us to act, let us be us and you be you. Us blacks did not ask to merger the two schools you racist whites need to ask your Republican Governor Deal about this buck stops at his office.

It's November 24, 2015, and the governor of Minneapolis said the video of police shooting is inconclusive. Video footage from the back of an ambulance does not appear to show conclusively what happened in the fatal shooting of an unarmed black man at Minneapolis police officer a week ago. Governor said on Monday about the video footage taken from the back of the ambulance does not appear to show it. The governor is trying to cover it up. If the ambulance was not there it's not going to show it. I have not read anywhere around when the shooting happened. So, governor you are going to have to tell a better lie than this. The governor said he has seen the tape. He told this at a news conference. It doesn't show anything would provide any confirmation to one point of view or another. Notice the governor has not mentioned anything about the videos in the police car or the officers. Come on man you are a governor of a state and the whole country can see you are trying to cover this up. The ambulance would have had to be on the scene when the shooting took place to video anything. Give up the videos and save the state a lot of money. You are going to be forced to give up those videos. This is making the police department look guilty. It will cost the department lots of dollars not to turn the tapes over.

I was looking at the news and the terrorists was talking about how this country is letting these police officers shooting the unarmed young black men and not doing anything about it. So, you see all those other countries are watching too. So, you see American you had better start handling your business. Don't someone is going to handle it for you. You know I said it once and I will say it again. Time goes by, but prejudice and racism is here to stay. Right over from where I live in Albany, Georgia, mostly run by blacks and you have whites always saying bad things about the elected officials. I don't think it is the rich whites. It's either the so called the middle class or the poor class they put stuff in the newspaper every day about the city and county officials. They put stuff in the paper every day like this the black lives matter. Folks need to focus their attention on where the real massacre of black lives is happening, Baltimore, Chicago. Black on black homicides are high in both cities. We as blacks know black lives matter. But do these gun happy coward police officers know? Why you would want to shoot an unarmed. When the first shot hit him, but do you keep on shooting? Don't' get me wrong. We have some good white folks down here, but they are more afraid than we are. The blacks and all their other brothers of color will join hands and stop all these unarmed brothers from being killed for no reason. I might not live to see it, but it's going to happen.

We as a black race of people should rejoice that justices are finally going to be served. Even though it is more than one year later, the white police officers that murdered the black 17-year-old in Chicago has been charged with murder. Laquan McDonald was killed by Officer Jason Van Dyke. This should have happened long ago it do not take this long to come up with videos. It's a shame that this country allows this to go on with law enforcement in the United States. Van Dykes became the first white police officer in Chicago in decades to be charged with murder for on duty use of lethal force and is in jail pending a second bond hearing on Monday, November 30, 2015. The new footage from the dashboard cameras on squad cars. Sent to renters and other media in response to public record request does not show the actual shooting. Why? Someone needs to explain why the camera do not show the shooting. Something is very wrong here. Why it took 13-month delay in charging Van Dyke and releasing the video. It taken 13 months to release a video with no shooting on it. Listen what CTU Vice President Jesse Sharkey said in a statement. We have to watch in anger and disappointment as the city has covered up police violence. He accused Mayor Rahm Emanuel of delaying release of the videos. The mayor should be charged. He was delaying release, so the shooting could be erased or taken out. Where is the shooting? If the cameras was running on the squad cars like they supposed to be where is the shooting part of the video.

What is all the fuss and debate about immigrants and refugees. We blacks and whites are immigrants. Read your history. Black ancestors was brought to this country against their will. Whites came from England and everywhere, so you can see we can't raise too much hell. Don't we might have to leave. This is America the land of the free and home of the brave. We as Americans we say have been letting people from other countries come here. I know it's about the terrorist but it's too late they are already over here. Some of the American people are trying to join so how are you going to stop it. What is needed is to protect our citizens from these American policies like the murders in Chicago and other cities in this country for the past 18 months. Listen what the creator of human kind Psalm 36:9. Therefore, he does not desire to see people die. Sadly, thought there are people who wickedly scheme to oppress and even kill others. God is telling us about what is going on in the world today. You can see it looks how people are being killed. Every time you pick up a paper someone has been killed and most of the time a law officer has killed or shot some young black man. Why are mostly every time a young black man is caught you have to choke him to him to death or shoot him. Why not taser him? Is it because they have that good old boy system in most of your Southern states? I think when you break the law you should be punished like anyone else because you wear the badge and you know better. But you know what there are officers where they can do what they want to people and hide behind that badge. I have seen officers lie in court.

I get so sick and tired of every time you pick up a newspaper you find articles where blacks are being talked about and put down by racist people who has nothing to do but keep up. Hell, I am 78 years old and love the United States. It makes me sick about what is happening to this country. Honestly morals love of this country have been replaced with greed, what is in it for me? It is unreal. Never in my life would I have realized this would happen to our great country. May our God help us. Until our leaders of this country get one accord and up hold the law for just one race of people. America is not going to get any rest. You see we are all God's children when he formed man from the dust of the ground all of the dust was the same color. Look at Genesis 1:26 where it say let's make man just read all of Genesis and I hope for all of you non Bible readers you will get something out of it. Because I can tell what kind of person you are by what you put in the newspaper you don't know Jesus. When you kill people like these police have been doing for the past 18 months and longer and the people like the prosecutors and judges call justified and an unarmed black man has been shot in the back. I would just say to these judges. You are going to be judged too. But not by man. No, its going to be by a higher power and all those bad seed you sowed you are going to reap them. You may get by down here but you will not get by God. I have learned to put God first in everything I do. I put my trust in God not man. Look what man is doing to God's children. He is murdering them unjustly. That's why we are having all these problems. Look at all those people who lost their lives. Look at all the terrorists trying to come over here and some are all ready over here. People's nothing but sin man cannot last long doing what he's doing God is going to cut him off.

It is December 1, 2015, and it is raining in the deep South. But nothing has changed for us blacks in America and no one seems to care. Not even in the Minneapolis. Four has been charged in the shooting of five protesters. Allen ScarSella 23 who was a prosecutor said in a complaint had admitted to opening fire on the five protesters, was charged with one count of second degree, riot while armed and five counts of second degree assault. What is wrong with the prosecutors when you are shooting someone you are trying to kill someone? These young white men were trying to kill those protesters just like the white officer killed the young black man. The same thing and the prosecutor knows it. Also charged Joseph Backman 27, Nathan Gustavsson 21 and Daniel Macey 26 were each charged with second degree riot in the November 23 late night shooting that left the five demonstrators all African American men aged 19 to 43 with wounds that were not life threatening. That don't mean anything. They were trying to kill these people. Hennepin County attorney Mike Freeman called the shooting racially motivated, and said additional charges are possible against the defendants and others. So now it's all out in the open. Now we can see how the prosecutors try to cover up stuff if an African American has been shot or murdered. It has been happening all the time. That's why blacks cannot get no justice in this country. In Tallahassee, Florida, September 28, 2006, the family of Martin Lee Anderson urged then Governor Jeb Bush on Wednesday to push for arrests in the January death of the teenager who was roughed up by guards at a Panama City book camp. The family's attorney, Ben Crump said he wanted to investigate completed before the November 7 general election. After November 7, who knows what will happen. Said Crump who is suing the Department of Juvenile Justice and Bay County Sherriff's Office for 40 million in the death of the 14-year-old boy. Security video tape taken at the camp showed a half hour encounter between Anderson and up to nine guard's who kicked and kneed him while a nurse watched. Anderson was formally declared dead several hours later at a Pensacola, Florida, hospital. The original autopsy said Anderson died of natural causes from complications of sickle cell, a normally benign blood disorder. A second autopsy found he was suffocated during this scuffle with the guards and Jeb Bush wants to be president. Blacks have not forgot what he done when he was governor of Florida.

 It is quiet in the deep South. Everyone is getting ready for Christmas. I hope and pray that we don't have any more killings of black men by police officers. You know it's true that the majority of American adults roughly three quarters still claim a religion and are more devout than they were a few years ago. It is a growing minority of American adults, mostly younger adults who say they don't belong to any organized faith. I am glad I am not one of the nones. My parents made Baptist faith and important part of my upbringing. You know this is why all of this stuff is happening in this country. America you has strayed away from God. You must be in one accord. Until this country put God in everything, we are not going anywhere. I don't care who get to be president. Its not going to work without God being involved. Because man has messed up and don't know how to fix it. The church promotes values that are good to have in a representative republic. When people stop believing in God, he said it's not that they believe in nothing. It's that they believe in anything. It is better to be hot or cold than lukewarm says the New Testament. Some of the nones atheists and agnostics are often hot as they actively try to seek truth but the lukewarm none are often wishy washy and that is not good for the republic.

Thank you, Jesus, for blessing me and my family.

9

Hope For The Future

It's December 2015. I hope and pray that 2016 will be better for every one especially for our young black men's in this country and someone put a stop to these coward police officers. Look at this Ohio grand jury clears police in fatal shooting of a 12-year-old on Monday December 28. The grand jury for weeks had been hearing testimony on the shooting of Rice. In November 2014, the 12-year-old Tamir Rice who was brandishing a toy gun at a park due to a lack of evidence indicating criminal activity. Someone needs to come up with a way to stop these unnecessary killings. Why would you want to shoot an armed man when he is running from you? Why can't you taser him? Why would you drive up and jump out of a car and shoot a 12-year-old kid without saying anything to him about putting the gun down? I have not read or heard on TV that the officers told the kid to put the gun down. They just drove up real fast and before the other officer could get out of the car, the other officer had shot this kid. The prosecutors said he don't see no evidence indicating criminal activity. The prosecutor don't want to see it. Why didn't the officers order the kid to put the gun down? If he would have he would have put it down. They did not do that. The prosecutor know that and he know those officers was wrong. I have not seen or read that he pointed the gun at them. So why did they kill that child? I am pretty sure that the officers and the prosecutor has kids. Just think all three of you. What if that had been your kid and a black officer killed him? I am pretty sure that the prosecutor would have found enough evidence to prosecute him. But once again that shows you this country has a double standard. If you are judged by the color of your skin. Don't let anyone fool you. I just sit back and listen at people talk and I can pretty much know what kind of person I am dealing with. I can tell all my people we are not loved in this country. Don't forget it. But God bless American.

Yes know 2015 went out with a lot of rain and storms and tornadoes and flooding in the deep South and very, very warm weather in December. Now those nonbelievers who don't read their Bible are afraid. But the word says before the end of time you cannot tell winter from summer. Only by the budding of the trees. Now we see it. Hot in December 87, temperatures flowers budding, peach trees putting out. People, all the signs are here. Look at all the rain, but he said it won't be rain but fire next time. Look at all the wars we are in. Look at the nations against one another. Look how the people are being paid to protect us are killing young black men. He is on his way back. He sees all the unjust that these so-called judges are doing, and God is not pleased with it. So, all you judges that has been judging unjustly, you will be judged by a higher power. That goes for all of those lying prosecutors to you will judge too. You know that's what I like about God. He don't see color because he made all of us. And he loves all of us the same. He do not love on no better than he do the other. We are all his children and he is our father who are in heaven. But somewhere along the way some of his children went contrary to what he said and are trying to play God and he is not going to put up with that. You know I am so glad that the God I serve is a just God. He looks beyond your faults and see yours needs. If we his people don't come together as one people. Listen in Deuteronomy 29:23 God destroyed four cities for the same sins that are going on today. Sodom, Gomorrah, Admah and Zeboi. The same thing and more are going on today. Homosexuality, men trying to change what God made and much more. That is not pleasing with God and he is going to stop it all. Pray for all the people in this book for their wrong doing. Thank you Jesus.

— The End —

Living in the Deep South is Hard and Dangerous

www.ingramcontent.com/pod-product-compliance
Lightning Source LLC
Chambersburg PA
CBHW052204110526
44591CB00012B/2076